I0082299

Hearth Dragons
Home-based Dragon Witchcraft

R.H. Marshall

GREEN MAGIC

Hearth Dragons © 2024 by R.H. Marshall.
All rights reserved. No part of this book may be
used or reproduced in any form without written
permission of the Author, except in the case of
quotations in articles and reviews.

GREEN MAGIC
Seed Factory
Aller
Langport
Somerset
TA10 0QN
England
www.greenmagicpublishing.com

Designed and typeset by Carrigboy, Wells, UK
www.carrigboy.co.uk

ISBN 978 1 915580 23 8

Author's word press address is: **rh-marshall.com**

GREEN MAGIC

Contents

This book is dedicated with love to

my Uncle John and to Bill,

who, as I wrote these pages,
were as brave as dragons.

Fly Free.

CHAPTER 1

Hearth Dragon Philosophy

THE AWAKENING OF THE HEARTH DRAGONS

In order to make positive changes in the world, we must first make positive changes to ourselves and our homes.

'As within – So without.'

One rainy morning, during the pandemic, the Hearth Dragon took flight in my mind. He came to me in a meditation, rising from the hearth and up, out of my house, and as he spread his wings to circle the neighbourhood, he also spread his love.

The more he circled and called, the more dragons rose from other houses. The sky was full of dragons, each one bringing the positive energy of love, care, gratitude and nourishment from its household and sharing it with the others.

The Hearth Dragon teaches us that big changes for the better in the world have to start in a small way. We are each responsible for the well-being of ourselves, our homes and our loved ones. By creating a positive environment at home and at work, we can cause a growing wave of healing throughout our communities and out further and further into the world.

Healing the world first begins with healing ourselves.

* * *

If you are reading this because of a feeling of growing unrest about the plight of the world and what the future holds for yourself and your family, then please know that you are not alone. Many of us feel concern and fear and a lack of control in these uncertain times. I created this book, with help from spirit guides and dragon guides, with a view to helping people take back some control of their own lives and swap fear for compassion. The dragons want you to understand your own power and know that every individual has the ability to make changes for the better.

I've always loved dragons. As a youngster, my mind created pictures of these giant creatures in deep slumber beneath tors and hills, and caves beneath the sea. They waited to re-awaken, when the time was right – when they were needed.

As I grew older, I heard of people who had worked with these beautiful beings from an astral dimension, but my understanding of them was limited and I was sceptical of things that could not be measured in an objective way.

I was, as many are, weighed down with the concept of what was 'real' and what could be 'proven'. Since then, as a spiritual medium, I have experienced things that science, as yet, cannot explain. I have realised also that we have a far greater number of senses than five, and that 'reality' is only ever 'real' to the individual, so there really is no point at all in getting caught up in that.

There are many dimensions, all around us. This material world is not as solid as we imagine and those experts in quantum physics will one day have the courage to explain this in terms of sub-atomic particles ... perhaps.

So, are dragons real?
Yes, they are ... and I know this because I have met many.
Subjectively ... but actually.

Some time ago, I attended a short weekend course in basic Shiatsu massage. The experience was a useful one in learning about the meridian energy lines of the body and about how to bring my own energy into a central place inside my body to be utilised through my hands. I learnt, interestingly, that the body's meridian lines are also known as dragon lines. Even more interestingly, I then found out that the Earth itself similarly has ley lines of energy that are also known as dragon paths.

If you check these lines out for yourself on the internet then you will notice how many ancient spiritual monuments have been built on these lines. A famous ley line, that of St. Michael, runs from Norfolk in the UK right down to St. Michael's Mount in Cornwall. It stretches from east to west across England. Along its path are numerous medieval Christian churches built in honour of St. Michael. I feel it's no coincidence that St. Michael was known to be a dragonslayer. Was this abundance of churches in his name an effort by medieval Christians to dilute the dragon energy of Pagan England? Whether this is the case or not, the very existence of these 'dragon paths' is evidence to me of the early belief of these mystical beings and their association with the Earth.

Modern science is a wonderful thing but it would have us believe that the wisdom and knowledge of ancient civilisations was less than our own. I disagree. Our species has learnt a great deal but has, I feel, forgotten so much more.

Recently, in the wake of the global pandemic and general unrest, there has been a shift in the energies of the Earth and in the consciousness of humans. There are many more followers of spiritual paths than there were even ten years ago. People are searching for something that has been lost to them. A necessary knowledge. A glimmer of hope that there really is 'more out there'. It's a hunger of the soul that every human feels at some point in their lives. It's an awareness of the mind and heart and the holistic unity that connects all things.

We have reconnected to the energy within ourselves and the Earth. We have reconnected to the dragons.

The dragon awakening is really our own awakening.

Those of us with a sensitivity to disruption have learnt not to take anything for granted. Nothing is safe. Nothing is 'ours'. We live in a very fragile world. As the cause of much of its fragility, we now need to strive to protect the balance of life. We cannot own this planet, this earthly dimension – we are merely passing through it.

Like many, I have found a deep peace and connection with the natural world and witchcraft has always been my way of finding a union with the energies of the Earth and of the spirit dimensions. Recently though, many of us have felt an increasing need to reach further towards healing the Earth, as well as ourselves. We've felt the pull of community and have needed to send positive thoughts that might nurture a kinder New Earth.

As a physical medium, my dealings with dragons have been tactile, as well as emotional and mental. They have the ability to enter our dreams, to evoke strong emotions in order for us to learn from them. They can gift us with clear mental images and colours. They can bring smells, information and strong gut feelings. Dragons can physically manifest too. They can produce shadows and movement, dancing lights, music and energy formations. Most of all, they bring a feeling of their and your own divine power, of love and completion.

Dragons make you aware of your own courage and ability, aware of your immortal spirit and your higher self.

I can feel Orphus as he sits within my own body. I feel his wings as they join the area between my shoulder blades. I feel his size, shape and weight, and the icy blast of his breath and the breeze caused by the beating of his wings.

In my mind, he shows me his pale skin and scales, horns and deep black eyes. He is small and lithe and talks to me of my quest for freedom.

He comes this close only when invited. This is important. Our own personal space is ours to govern.

Orphus was the name he gave me to call and know him by. He lives in snow-capped mountains and has known me (he tells me) since we met when I was a child and would wander in my daydreams to far-off lands.

He is my magickal companion, along with other dragons and spirit guides, who aids me in my energy work and my journeys. They lament with me in my woes and rejoice with me in my celebrations.

Orphus has instructed me to write this book so I can share his wisdom with you, because if you are here, reading this, then you are blessed as someone who is interested enough to want to make positive changes to themselves, their lives and the world at large.

There have been many books written about dragon magick. Many are excellent. Most deal with dragon energy work in a manner that uses tools and rituals akin to those of 'high magick'. There is much use of swords and elaborate chants and formal clothing. I have a deep respect for this style of magick but you won't find any of that in this book. I've always preferred a quieter, less theatrical approach to my witchcraft. It is largely based on Earth energies and the use of trance, and I've found this means of working with dragons to be most effective and powerful.

There is no one way to work with dragons. We can but give you information enough to help you make a confident start on your own magickal journey. You will, with time, adopt your own methods of working that suit you and your dragon friends.

THE ASPIRATIONS & CREED

There are certain guidelines of thought and conduct that need to be acknowledged when working with dragons ... they won't just work with anybody, you know. They don't stand any nonsense from bullish types or those out to harm others. Dragons, I have learnt, will happily add their own brand of harmonious magick to yours to help you improve yourself, or improve your health, your relationships, or make yourself more financially comfortable. They do this, not because they feel you need riches or beauty or the affection of others but because in helping you be free of worry and suffering, you are more able to get on with the important task of healing the world.

Healing the world means different things to different people. For the purposes of this book, I refer to the ascension of the New Earth. A New Earth that is greener and kinder. Soil, seas, rivers and skies that are unpolluted, rain that is safe to drink, food that is wholesome and grown without chemicals, people free to live in peace, animals able to roam and be free of cruelty – communities of people that help each other, support each other and the growing spiritual awareness that we, humans, every one of us, are accountable for what we create within ourselves and within our world.

Dragons, like people, value respect, humility, moderation, creativity, happiness, courage of conviction, balance, harmony and honesty.

'Truth' is a difficult virtue in our society. Being true to ourselves, especially. So much of what we feel is right has to be kept hidden and disguised for fear of ridicule and hatred.

Speaking personally, I have received hurtful comments and mail from strangers and even family because of my mediumship, beliefs and way of life and I know that many of you will have suffered the same. Feel better in the knowledge that you have a chance of wonderful liberation because of the openness of your mind and heart. So many, sadly, will never know this joy.

Another important and often overlooked aspect in magickal work, and life generally, is the need to have fun. Dragons love a bit of a frolic, and human beings work and thrive so much better when they are enjoying themselves. So, whilst working with dragon energy and saving the world is a serious, important business, remember to seek pleasure in life and work. Your magickal vibration will be so much higher and lighter if you don't take yourself and daily situations too seriously.

Working with incarnate entities can, at first, be a little strange. You will most likely feel like you are talking to yourself and you may also feel a little foolish – but persevere. The dragons will make themselves known to you. You will find, within these pages, guidance in meditation and trance which will open and finely-tune your communication skills, with some practice. Each person has a unique way of creating communication with their guides. Have faith in them and have faith in yourself. Faith and trust go a long way to bridging the great gap between dimensions.

Before you do any energy work, witchcraft or whatever you want to call it, it will help to recite the Creed (the one below or your own creation, based on your aspirations) to assist you in being clear in your mind of the bigger picture. The Creed is the overview of your work ... the Great Intent ... after this you can open or cast your Circle and add your personal and specific intentions for your spell, healing or ritual.

THE HEARTH DRAGONS CREED

> We bind and work as one,
> In kindness, faith and fun.
> To heal, to nourish ourselves, our hearth.
> To heal and nurture
> our kinder New Earth.

When I work with my fellow witch and friend, we always sing this in harmony to a beautiful tune that she created for it. When I work alone, I still sing it. In my experience, magickal chants which have tunes have a very positive effect on the energy of the Circle. Music is a catalyst of success within magick as it has a high vibration; and when there is more than one person involved in the work, the music will focus and unite your thoughts and combine your own personal energies.

You may choose to work alone with your dragons or you may choose to work with others. If you choose to work with others then my advice is to choose carefully. Energies can easily be put off-balance when a less committed or sceptical personality is put into the mix. On this occasion, 'less is more'.

My last word here is to enjoy your journey. Learn to fly with your dragon. Embrace the freedom of your friendships with them and you will find that every aspect of your life can improve.

CHAPTER 2

Dragon Communication

IMPORTANT NOTE: if you are suffering from mental illness, be kind to yourself and get professional help and healing. Working with dragons and spirits is beneficial for our lives when we are balanced and healthy, but I would advise not to attempt communication with any other dimension if you are unwell. By all means, use the grounding energies of nature and the elements to help heal yourself, but stay clear of astral communication.

MEET YOUR DRAGON GUIDE – A MEDITATION

Before you embark on any of the dragon meditations, rituals and spells in this book, you will need to supply yourself with an A5 notebook that can be used as your magickal journal. You can use this journal to record facts, feelings, thoughts and ideas as you embark on your journey of learning and working with dragons.

For this meditation, you will need your magickal journal, a pen, a comfortable chair or bed and loose clothing to wear.

Make sure you've used the bathroom and that you are clean and in a positive frame of mind.

Have some pre-prepared refreshments ready in the form of a snack and a drink for after the meditation.

Read this meditation through, then settle yourself in your quiet, comfortable space, where you won't be disturbed, and replay the journey in your mind.

If you have a trusted friend who can read it out to you whilst you relax then all the better. Maybe you could take it in turns to meet your dragons.

During the meditation, before you invite your dragon in, I will ask you first to invite your spirit guide to stay near you. This guide has probably been with you all your life and will only allow helpful entities to draw close to you. Trust your guide, even if you have not been aware of their presence before. A spirit guide will take good care of you if invited to do so. You want to ensure that any astral being you invite into your personal space has your best interest at heart. Your spirit guide will oversee this and act as a gatekeeper. You may be able to sense your guide with you. Even if you cannot, know that if you call, they will always come.

First, relax your body by breathing deeply and slowly for a few minutes. Let your thoughts come and go but try to return your focus to your breath.

From head to toe, in turn, tense and relax your muscles, keeping your breath slow and deep. Tense and relax your scalp muscles, your face … your chin and neck. Shoulders … arms … hands … chest … abdomen … stomach … sides … back … bottom … groin … thighs … calves … feet … and toes.

Close your eyes and imagine roots reaching out from your body down into the earth. Feel the coolness of the earth as you penetrate the soft soil. This is your masculine self pushing into the ground. Reach down as you breathe out, and as you breathe in pull the earth energy up into your body. This is your feminine self, receiving and containing. Pull it into your limbs and your solar plexus. This yogic exercise will help keep your energies balanced and anchored before you embark on your meditation.

Breathe deeply, in and out … and let the earth energy circulate through your body.

Now, with your eyes still closed, form a mental image of the place you are resting in. Try to remember the details of the room that you are physically in. Feel the temperature, warm or cool upon your skin. Breathe in the smells of the room and yourself. These may be subtle or strong. What noises can you hear?

See the room clearly in your mind … the window, door, furniture. Visualise the colours, textures and patterns. The decor on the walls, the floor, the electrical devices, sockets and cables, the personal paraphernalia. It is forming clearly in your mind.

Now focus again on your own breath, your own body, feel your hands, your limbs, your clothing. In your mind, you can see yourself relaxing and reclining in the room. You see your own feet and fingers.

Breathe deeply and slowly and visualise a golden light shining onto your face. It spreads and embraces your body entirely with its warm rays. It feels like a soft hug and fills you with peace.

When you are ready, invite in your Spirit Guide and Gatekeeper. Anyone who embarks on any kind of mediumship will acquire a special spirit guide who acts as a gatekeeper for yourself and your Circle. Say out loud:

> I ask my spirit guide to remain with me as gatekeeper whilst I sit to communicate with dragons of the astral dimension. I thank them for their protection.

Then invite in your dragon by saying:

> I sit with intention to communicate. I sit with love, light and positive energy and work only for the highest good.
>
> I invite my dragon friend and guide to draw close to me.

Wait now for any sign that the dragon may give you of evidence of its presence. Do not rush. Patience is key.

When you feel ready to move on with more communication ask your dragon to show you a colour that represents it.

Then request a colour that represents you.

When your dragon has helped you visualise the colour, thank it, acknowledge that you have seen it and ask that the meaning of these colours be explained.

Let the communication unfold naturally and at the dragon's own pace.

Talk to it, ask it to show itself to you, ask if it might give you a name to call it by. Ask your dragon to give you a means to identify it, so that you can recognise when it is near.

Get to know how your dragon feels. Pay attention to physical sensations and temperature changes, to unexpected sounds and smells and any information landing in your mind.

Spend as long as you need, getting to know your dragon guide. Enjoy this initial meeting for what it is, a means of introduction.

When you are ready to say farewell to your dragon, just thank it for coming and ask that it step away and allow you to return to your normal state of consciousness.

Take your time.

Allow the dragon to depart.

Become aware again of your room and your body, wiggle your fingers and toes. Take a refreshing breath or yawn. Your heart rate will have slowed down during the meditation and yawning will help oxygenate and revive you. Open your eyes and smile.

Thank your spirit guide for the help and support provided. Ask your guide to help you close down, energetically, and allow you to continue your day in a normal, earthly way.

Grab yourself a cup of tea, coffee or glass of water and eat something. This will ground you and restore you mentally and physically.

These refreshments will become an enjoyable, habitual, closing-down ritual after any energy work.

When you are done you can record any valuable information, notions and experiences from the meditation in your magickal journal.

Congratulations if you managed to meet your dragon. Don't worry if you didn't. This exercise can be repeated as many times as necessary. Communication with incarnate beings takes a lot of practice. It took me two years to be able to recognise and communicate successfully with my spirit guide, but all that practice helped me connect quickly with my dragon guide when the time came.

It can take just a moment, or weeks, months or years to become proficient at this kind of mediumship. Think of your body as a fine instrument that you need to take care of and practice tuning and working with in order to get the best results.

If you just can't get any mental or physical evidence of the dragon's presence from this exercise then that doesn't mean it isn't around. Continue with your preparations for working with your dragon. Dragons can communicate in many ways. If you and your dragon are serious about wanting to work together, a means of transferring information to you will be found, a few of which I will talk about later.

It all takes time and dedication.

MUSIC & DANCE

If you are anything like me, you have glanced at this title and inwardly groaned at the prospect of having to sing or dance. Books of a spiritual nature seem to be filled with people enjoying this particular form of magick. And it is indeed a most powerful source of energy. I am a terrible singer and an even worse dancer. I envy those of you who are lithe of body and harmonious in voice. You already have an advantage in raising your vibration in a beautiful and creative way. I suggest those of you who are able to enjoy this form of magick do so in abundance. Open your Circles with eager movement and song.

I have already mentioned that I do, in fact, sing my opening Creed. I didn't tell you that I sing it rather badly. But that doesn't matter. I sing it with sincerity and with passion and the words rise and enter the universe, filling the air with their intent. My friend and fellow witch has a beautiful and powerful singing voice. When she sings the Creed with me the hair stands up on my arms and the song tingles through my blood.

Music can affect us like a drug. That is why it has such vigorous magick of its own.

Each person has their own response to music. Each person is affected by different kinds of music and even if you are one of the rarest personalities that doesn't like music, I expect you can still appreciate the sounds of nature, rain on window glass, wind in leaves, waves on the seashore, the call of wolves, whales, birds etc. This is all music. The dictionary defines it as 'organised sound'.

For our purposes, music is simply sound that causes us to feel.

Using music with magick is like adding a catalyst. It accelerates the energy by causing an emotion within us and creating vibrational sound waves in the universe.

If you have ever read about the water memory experiments by the Japanese scientist, Masaru Emoto, then you will be aware of his work with frozen water and sound. He found the vibration of words and sound could change the crystal structure within the water. Disharmonious sound, caused disharmonious crystal patterns, while harmonious sound created beautiful symmetrical patterning to occur.

For our purposes, the lesson here is that sound can also change the harmony of the water within us and the water in the atmosphere. We have the potential to heal or hurt ourselves, others, and the world around us by the words and sounds we use.

Water Dragons will be very aware of this, I'm sure.

Music can also change our conscious state. The right music can send us deeply into meditation and trance and aid our communication with those of other dimensions.

My own personal experience of this is that the louder the music, especially drumming, the deeper into trance I will become. I will talk more about the use of trance with you later.

It's no coincidence then that cultures throughout human history have used music and dance in religious and spiritual ceremonies where communication with ancestors and astral dimensions was necessary.

So, although I'm an awkward Brit with no sense of rhythm, I encourage you, if you are able, to dance within your rituals and allow the energy of your movement and the pulsing of your blood to sing through your body and increase the power of your work. Sing your Creeds, sing your spells, play instruments, put your Spotify tracks on or use the music of nature to enhance your spells.

Dragons love music. They will probably gambol around with you and if you are very lucky you may even hear their own music and songs. Music is a direct way to a dragon's heart and it can unite you both in the way it unites a choir of humans. Imagine how much can be achieved with such a union. One lone voice can be beautiful but a whole choir in harmony can lift your spirit above the clouds.

With music and dance you and your dragon can create exquisite synergy.

TRANCE

For much of your work with dragons, be it meditation, dancing or ritual, you will probably find yourself in a state of trance. Trance is merely an altered state of consciousness. It can be as light as a daydream state, like when you are busy doing some household task that doesn't require concentration, or it can be very deep, drug-like, or to the point of the medium being only semi-conscious, as often happens during physical mediumship Circles.

Trance is a useful tool for communication with entities not from this earth because it helps us rid ourselves of the awareness of this material world. It slows our heart rate, helps us relax and opens a gateway for communication beyond our worldly senses.

A light trance state is really all that is necessary for day-to-day work with dragons. This can be achieved by using the relaxation and slow, deep breathing exercise described in the first Chapter's meditation. You may find, as I do, that certain kinds of music will heighten your trance state. I find a strong, tribal drum beat to be a very powerful way to 'lose myself'. Mostly, for work as a connector to the spirit world, my guide and spirit team can render me nearly unconscious, so that can they affect physical phenomena without it bothering me in the slightest.

During healing work with dragons, my spirit guide can nudge me, my conscious self, aside so that a dragon can work through me to bring aid to a human third party. I am still aware of what is happening but I feel a little detached.

Anyone can do this, if they have the will and the time to practice.

Everyone will develop a different way of working with these beings and your own levels of trance will happen quite naturally as you progress. The second you invite a dragon to come close to you your conscious state will alter in some way.

You don't need to worry about causing this or hindering this. Just let it happen. Your body and mind will adapt and respond according to your own intentions and the needs of your dragon companion. If at any time you feel uncomfortable with the changes occurring, you can ask them to stop. You are in control here and nothing happens without your invitation.

I advise you not to take or smoke substances that will artificially change your consciousness when working with dragons. If you do so you cannot properly gauge the effects of dragon energy. Keep your mind and your body as clean as possible. It will be far easier for dragons to work through you and with you if your blood is not contaminated with drugs.

The Dragon Wing Tea and Dragon Dream Tea recipes in Chapter 10, are the only substance I would recommend. The teas are safe and nourishing. They will relax you without adding toxins to your body and brain.

Trust that your spirit helpers and your dragon friends will work in a way that will best facilitate the intention of the work and will find the best way to work with you for the benefit of all concerned.

DREAMS AND DREAM RITUAL

Dragons are adept at entering dreams. They will do so when they are trying to get your attention or trying to inform you of something.

You can invite them to work with you in your dream state by using a simple dragon dream ritual before you go to bed.

Intention: Communication with dragons in your dreams.
Moon Phase: Dark or waning moon.

You will need:

- Dragon Dream Tea.
- A warm bath.
- Cosy pyjamas.
- A small drawstring bag (your Dragon Dream Bag).
- Your magickal journal.
- Crystal: Moonstone.
- Dried Herbs: Mint, camomile, lavender, mugwort.
- Oils and Teas: Dragon Dream Tea.

THE RITUAL

First, prepare some Dragon Dream Tea using the recipe in Chapter 10.

Put some of the tea herbs (mint, camomile, lavender and mugwort) and the moonstone in the dragon dream bag and keep some by in a dish to add to your bath.

Don't eat too much during the day before and don't eat anything at all at least 4 hours before sleep. This stops your body from working overtime trying to digest food and keeping you from sleeping properly. Don't consume alcohol or too much caffeine during the day or evening. Drink plenty of filtered water all day and sip it during the evening to keep yourself hydrated, and free of toxins, but your bladder is not over-full.

Just before you go to bed use some of the herbs you have prepared for your tea and add them to a warm, relaxing bath. Whilst in the bath ask the water to heal you of the day's stresses and strains and to ease any aches and pains.

Then close your eyes, relax and say:

> I prepare my mind and body for tonight's sleep.
> May I sleep well and peacefully and may my dragon companions visit my dreams to increase my knowledge and wisdom.
> May I recall any useful information with clarity, upon waking.

Get yourself ready for bed in comfortable nightwear and ensure you have clean, soft bedding. Make your Dragon Dream Tea.

As you sip it repeat the spoken intention that you used in the bath.

Put the dream bag full of the dry or fresh tea herbs under your pillow and repeat the spoken intention for the third time.

Don't watch anything negative on the TV or on your phone in the evening. Fill your mind only with beautiful, light information that will give you pleasure and a sense of well-being.

Settle yourself into a wonderful, restful sleep and in the morning write all your dream information in your magickal journal in as much detail as you can remember. Sometimes, even the most trivial detail can later be understood to have value.

If you don't remember your dreams then it's likely the information has gone into your subconscious and may well be remembered at a later date.

If at any time you feel uncomfortable about a situation whilst dreaming then you can call upon it to stop. Even in dreams, we can have control over what happens. Be strong and stop the proceedings by placing your palm outwards in front of you and demanding the action stop. You will no doubt wake up at this point.

All my dream communication with dragons has been informative and uplifting but dragons are dragons and they can sometimes seem rather intimidating. I met an enormous black dragon once in my dream. She towered above me and looked utterly fearsome. She looked down at me and told me to find my courage for only then could I pursue my chosen path. She was right.

Dragons will tell you what you need to hear and they won't make it pretty or fluffy. Be prepared for plain speaking and learn to be tenacious in dealing with such truths.

SCRIPTS FOR WORKING WITH DRAGONS

It isn't necessary to have a special script when working with dragons, but it can be rewarding for you and your dragon guide to create your own unique alphabet for use in your work together. There are also books that contain certain 'dragon scripts' that you may like to research and use, or you can, as Orphus and I do, use the witch's Theban script. We use this because it's so very beautiful and carries an interesting history. It is a substitution cipher of Latin script and was said to have been used by early witches during the medieval witch hunts of Europe to write secret letters to each other.

I would have thought this was more likely to alert the witch hunters to their identity so I feel that the script was possibly used for ritual work.

Theban Script

A	B	C	D	E

F	G	H	I & J	K

L	M	N	O	P

Q	R	S	T	U

V	W	X	Y	Z

I use the script in my grimoire and my tools and spells to add the vibration of words and beauty to our work. It's a way of creating more energy. Any effort on your part to cherish, respect and enjoy your magick will enhance its outcome.

The Theban script added here is my own hand-written copy of the script found in *Polygraphia*, 1518, by Johannes Trithemius.

SIGILS

Sigils are symbols that are created to condense a visual prompt of your intention.

They can be created by you and your dragon or you can use pre-made sigils for convenience and ease.

They are useful for bringing the intention to mind very quickly and for adorning tools used in the spell. They can be added to spell jars and bags and burnt in release rituals. They can also be drawn in the air when you need to do magick quickly and spontaneously. I suggest you try to memorise your sigils for this reason.

Think of a sigil as a poem. A piece of lengthy prose can be a beautiful thing. But a poem has a unique way of using select, minimal and powerful language to communicate the writer's concept.

A sigil contains the undiluted energy of your spell.

When creating sigils for work with dragons you may want to ask your dragon to help inspire you. My dragon loves to be involved and help me in my art and my writing. They enjoy the energy of artistic pursuits and will ride the waves of creativity that you both produce.

SIGILS

FOR DRAGON WITCHCRAFT

LOVE & HARMONY

PROTECTION & SAFETY

CREATIVITY & FERTILITY

HEALING

ABUNDANCE & PROSPERITY

RELEASE

SUCCESS & OPPORTINITY

BANISH

ATTRACT

STUDY /MEDITATION & COMMUNICATION

FLYNG & JOURNEYING

One simple technique of creating sigils is to write your intention as a sentence, either in your usual alphabet or using your chosen magickal script. Then reduce the sentence to keywords. Then reduce further until you only have two words that sum up the intention. Take out all the vowels and arrange the remaining consonants into a pleasing form and symbol.

Or, if you are artistic, you can draw an image that represents your intention. Simplify it until it is easily memorable.

If you are very lucky, your dragon might download a design straight into your head and save you the effort!

The sigils in the included table are created from Theban Script. I use two words in the intention and use the first letter of each. I draw the Theban letter for each and then combine it into one symbol.

However you choose to create your sigil ensure that it is not so elaborate that you can't easily keep it in your mind or reproduce it on candles and tools, etc.

DRAGON SCRYING MIRROR & TRANSFIGURATION

I refer to transfiguration here, not as the shapeshifting of Professor McGonagall's class in the Harry Potter books (although that would indeed be something to write about!) but to the energy formations created by spirit and dragon entities.

Your dragons, when invited and should they feel inclined, are able to create an energy form of their own countenance over your own face. The substance looks similar to a heat haze but when stabilized can form features. This can be seen in an ordinary mirror but is clearest in a dark mirror in a dimly lit room or a room with a dim red lamp. It sounds creepy but I assure you the reasons for this are scientific.

The substances used are just not visible in direct light. I have experimented with every kind of light and tried to see it in every kind of reflected surface but half-light and a scrying mirror is best. I'm convinced that the reason witches of old used this tool in twilight or candlelight is for the very same reason.

I have many years of experience in transfiguration. Mostly in my work with my spirit team and then after with the dragons, who worked with the spirit teams.

It takes practice, dedication and some courage. The process isn't at all dangerous. It is beautiful and often breathtaking, but at first, it can be a little shocking to the uninitiated because the human brain is seeing things that it cannot compute. The first time you see your dragon's image over your own face your heart may jump and race. It is a unique and life-changing experience. This kind of first-hand, physical experience, will dissolve any doubt of the 'reality' of astral beings.

It takes a while for the dragons to master transfiguration as they need to be able to balance your and their energies and create a recognisable form. So, the exercise below will need to be practiced and practiced. I guarantee that once you have successfully seen a transfigured image of your dragon and your brain has got used to the idea, you will want to try it again and again.

Transfiguration, done well, is truly one of the most awesome things I have ever witnessed.

To see your dragon transfigure, you will need:

- A scrying mirror (see Chapter 3 on how to make one, or what to buy).
- A dimly lit room (a dim red lamp works well, twilight, or a soft night light).
- Your magickal journal.
- Pre-prepared refreshments for after the exercise.
- Wear comfortable, loose clothing of a dark material.
- Relaxing music.

You may want to try this exercise with a trusted friend if it helps make you feel more comfortable, especially the first time you try this.

Prepare your refreshments of a snack and a drink in advance to partake in after your experience.

Set up your room with your dim lighting (you will need to experiment with this to find out what works best for visibility ... too bright and you won't see the transfiguration energy ... too dim and you won't see anything at all. It's tricky and takes practice).

Put some clothes on that are comfortable and non-restrictive. You will need to enter a light trance state for this and you don't want to be suddenly brought back to alertness by a pinching bra or trouser waistband. Wear dark clothing so that bright colours won't detract and distract from viewing the subtle energy changes.

Remove any shiny, metal items from your attire because these will cause reflective light and confuse your vision of the energy image.

Put some music on that helps you relax.

Remove your spectacles if you wear them as they will reflect light and obscure the energy image.

Don't wear heavy makeup or anything that is going to dominate in the reflective image. You don't want to see your dragon in bright red lipstick and false eyelashes. Your face needs to recede and blur. It is a tool of conductivity only.

Have your dark mirror to hand.

When you are ready and sitting comfortably and are sure not to be disturbed by people and devices you can begin the meditation.

Say out loud:

> I ask my spirit guide to remain with me as gatekeeper whilst I sit to communicate with dragons of the astral dimension.

I thank them for their protection.

Then invite in your dragon by saying:

> I sit with intention to communicate. I sit with love, light and positive energy and work only for the highest good.
>
> I invite my dragon friend and guide to draw close to me and transfigure their own image for me to see.

Close your eyes and breathe deeply, let your mind absorb the music and let your thoughts come and go. Drift away with the music. Register the changes in temperature, the sounds and the physical sensations. Register, then let the information go. Just be. For the length of two tracks of music, just sit quietly. You will be entering a state of trance. This may be a very light or mid-trance. You may feel slightly drunk and sleepy. This is normal. Just let it happen.

Slowly open your eyes and look into the scrying mirror. Keep your breath steady and stay relaxed. You are perfectly safe. You may see a white hazy, substance in front of your face. This is a good sign that the experiment is working.

You may also feel your body temperature starting to rise during the meditation. This is normal and is caused by the high vibration of the energies being used. If it feels too hot, just tell your dragons and spirit guides and they will cool things down for you.

When you look into the mirror you may, at first, just see the quiver of a hazy energy over your own face. It may be clear or whitish or sometimes it has dark blobs. Gradually (and it may not happen on your first try), the energy will stabilise and start to form features. If you are very lucky, you will start to see your dragon's face form over your own. Stay calm. Your own face is not being changed. It is just an energy covering. You may, if you look down, even see your hands changing. If at any time you feel uncomfortable, just ask your dragon to step back, otherwise just enjoy the show.

The transfigured energy will probably only last a few minutes. It may not happen at all. This kind of energy work is very advanced and can take years of practice to create. Remember always that your team of dragons and guides will most likely have to learn new skills alongside you, so have patience. Stay respectful and grateful of what they have achieved and are trying to achieve. Stay upbeat and encouraging and have faith and trust in them.

When you are finished, say:

I thank my spirit guide, dragons and helpers for all they have achieved.

I ask that they close me down now so that I can return to my normal routine.

Farewell to you all and thank you for your continued protection.

Now you can put the lights on, eat your refreshments and record the experience in your journal.

If this kind of close encounter isn't your cup of tea, then that's absolutely fine. Not everyone wants or needs to try this level of communication.

If you don't want to try transfiguration, then just skip this section and you can continue with the other rituals and spell work that don't require direct contact of this nature.

If, like me, you have an insatiable curiosity and need to try all sorts of weird and wonderful things, then you will enjoy this very much.

ORACLE & TAROT CARDS

Divination cards can be a useful way to stay connected with your dragons on a daily basis.

Your dragon may be interested in helping out with full readings for yourself and others or you could just ask for assistance in picking out a single daily card to give you an idea of what to expect that day.

Orphus and I have a daily routine of picking a card from the oracle deck. I shuffle the cards and hold them in my hand. I ask him to give me a number, between 1 and the number of cards I'm holding, that will give me guidance for the day ahead.

He always shows himself to me in my mind as I shuffle. His long white snout and closely set, almond-shaped black eyes. Then a number pops into my head and is repeated over and over. I count through the cards from the top of the pile and put the card chosen on the table next to my altar. I ponder the card, thank him, and then get on with my day. At the end of the day, I write in my magickal journal what the day brought and how it related to the card.

There are different ways of doing this, some people spread the cards and pass their hand over them until they feel a sensation. Some people fan the cards and pick one and some like to shuffle and see what pops out. You may be able to just cut the deck and know that the card you turn over will be the right one.

It's a simple and quick exercise that keeps you in the practice of communication. It's also quite useful to know what might arise before you get there. Dragons are very accurate in their ability to choose cards and I'm always a little amazed by this.

DRAGON PENDULUM DIVINATION

One great thing about pendulums is that they are so portable. They can also be very beautiful. I have to say that in the past I've not actually been very good at using them. They tended to quiver and dance uncontrollably on one spot but since I've been working with dragons, I've found that I can channel their energy to good effect.

There are some lovely pendulums that can be purchased made from crystals, metals and wood. I've tried a selection of them over the years but now I use my dragon protective amulet, which is a silver necklace with a dragon wrapped around a turquoise stone.

You can really use anything as long as it is suspended, can swing and has a good weight to it. Your pendulum will, over time, absorb your energy and that of your dragon. For this reason, it's best not to let other people use it so that you can maintain its balance and harmony.

When using the pendulum, keep your intention or question in mind. Connect with your dragon by saying:

Dragon Guide, the truth I seek.
Through pendulum, your truth can speak.

Hold it over your divination board or use the Hearth Dragon board illustration included here. Let the pendulum swing of its own accord. Do not force the movement. Your dragon will need practice to be able to channel energy through you to swing the pendulum in answer to questions. Up and down for 'yes'. Side to side for 'no'; and diagonally, each way, for 'maybe' and 'rephrase'.

When you are practiced in this you will no longer require a board to be able to read the movement of the pendulum.

Remember that the answers are only your dragon's honest opinion. Ultimately, you must decide for yourself what the truth of the matter is.

You can also use the pendulum as a dowsing tool to find the dragon path ley lines in your area. There are many and they are worldwide. You can use it as you walk around an area or hold it over a map. You will become acquainted with its movement and quirks as if it were a live being. Experiment and remember to always keep a focus on your intention while you use it.

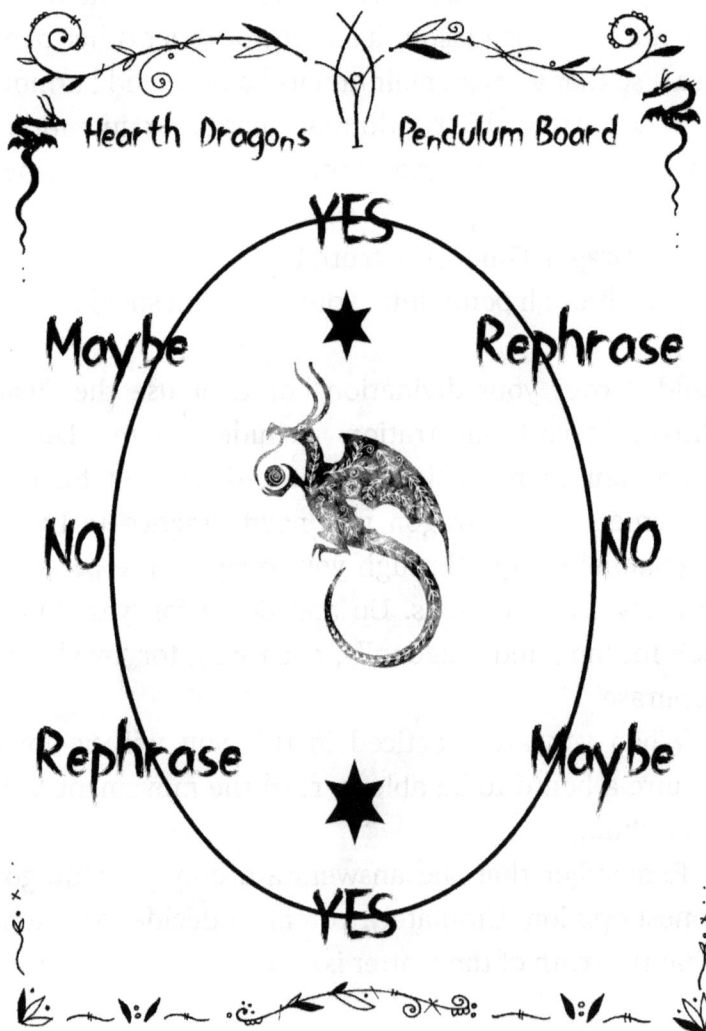

Hearth Dragons   Pendulum Board

YES

Maybe

Rephrase

NO

NO

Rephrase

Maybe

YES

CHAPTER 3

Tools & Rituals

Magickal tools are as individual as you are. Recently, witchcraft has seen a rise in interest and so has also become an area of commercial abundance. It is easier now than ever before to buy gorgeous items for your altar. It is, however, unnecessary to spend lots of money. You can find much of what you need in nature, especially for element representations. I made my own wand from an offered branch of my silver birch tree, and my water element is a piece of dried seaweed and a shell that my husband gave to me from our holiday beach ramble.

You can inscribe or paint your tools with your dragon script symbols or sigils.

TOOLS FOR THE ALTAR

Altar base – You can use a cloth or a tray or just a table or dresser top.

I try to make the altar as colourful, shiny and engaging as I can. Both for myself and for the dragons, who love to use colour in their communication.

Element of Fire – Candles –

I use two tea lights, one black and one white, for balance. But it's also nice to use coloured candles to represent the thing you are trying to manifest. Orange for luck, red for happiness or passion, blue and lilac for calmness and healing, green for money, purple for knowledge and divination and psychic work, pink for love, self-care and friendship and yellow for uplifting the spirit, bringing courage, confidence and general well-being.

Do not leave any candles unattended.

Element of Water – Dishes, bottles or a chalice of water, bowl of water-related objects –

If you are able to visit a beach, then pick up some lovely pebbles, sea glass, driftwood, etc., which will look and feel great on your altar.

Element of Air – Incense, an empty glass bottle, feathers –

Incense sticks and cones are useful to create a lovely ambience in the room, and as well as providing a tool for purification, the smoke represents the element of air. What type of incense you want to use is a personal choice. I like Dragon's Blood because it smells gorgeous and the name of it gives it an obvious link with dragon energy.

Be careful if you have pets around and people with asthma or breathing problems of any kind. Don't burn any incense for too long or too regularly. Research your incense and pick those that are safe for you and your family. As with candles, do not leave them unattended.

Element of Earth – Crystals, salt, rocks or plants –

A list of crystals and uses can be found in Chapter 7. Salt is a good purifier and is useful to have around for protection spells, healing and purification spells. I like to use Himalayan salt and sea salt. You can also add cut flowers or small houseplants to your altar if you have room. Rocks and wood are freely accessible items. As long as it feels good to you then use it.

Element of Spirit – Dragon image –

This can be a statue, a picture, a piece of jewellery ... as long as it represents a dragon that you find an affinity with, then it can be used. It will help you focus on dragon energy. A visual reminder of your intended channel is always helpful.

Offering Bowl – This is just a small bowl for offerings to your dragons as a means of a thank you for their help. It's a symbol of gratitude and can make a big difference to your relationship with your dragon. An offering strengthens your bond and the notion of 'give and take' and mutual respect.

Dragons all have particular tastes, like humans, so take some time to meditate and find out what your dragon would most appreciate. Orphus likes white flowers, milk or bread and honey. Sometimes I will use seeds that I will later plant. This is especially lovely if the plants, when grown, can be used in the rituals.

WORKING TOOLS

Wand –

There are so many lovely wands that can be bought online, or you can make your own. Wands are used to channel energy from source to objects. They are an extension of you. You can use your hand also but a wand can be adapted for specific purposes and provide a point of focus. Any tool that is hand-crafted will be imbued with extra energy and purpose.

Bell –

Any small bell with a clear, clean ringing tone is good. I use Tibetan bells. Bells are rung to cleanse and purify the space and objects by replacing negative vibrations with positive ones. A bell can also be used to mark the beginning and end of your ritual.

Book of Shadows, Grimoire or Energy Work Book or Folder –

To keep your spells, correspondences and ritual information at hand and ready to use. You may find that you want to modify my own and other people's guidance regarding working with dragons. Make sure you keep a written record.

Magickal Journal –

To record details and outcomes of spells, and ideas and thoughts, and also to write down oracle or tarot card readings.

Compact Mirror – or a small mirror with a case –

This is for shadow work and will have a dual purpose. Before you use the mirror for shadow work, you can also turn it into a talisman of safety and grounding during the Dragon Island meditation.

Dark Scrying Mirror – for transfiguration and divination –

You can use obsidian or just paint some card black and put it behind some glass and into a frame. Black water bowls can be used but are at the wrong angle for transfiguration as you need to be able to see your own reflection.

Dragon Oracle or Tarot –

It's beneficial to have dragon-themed cards to focus on dragon guidance. You can use these as a daily guide or as a means to answer specific queries. Call in your dragon guide to help you. Choose cards that look and feel attractive to you.

An Oil Burner –

Use scented dragon oils to bring focus and clarity to your mind.

Herbs –

Dry or fresh. A small list of herbs that can be used for the dragon energy exercises in this book can be found in Chapter 7.

Oils & Teas –

A list of oils for dragon work and how to make them can be found in Chapter 10.

Dragon Dream Bag –

A small drawstring bag to contain your herbs and crystals for dream work. This can be as simple or decorative as you like. If you are a crafter, you can make your own, otherwise a purchased small gift or soap bag will be perfect.

Spell Bags –

Small drawstring bags to fill with herbs, crystals and sigils for some of your spells.

Pendulum –

You can buy a pendulum, make one, or use a piece of hanging jewellery, like a necklace. See Chapter 2 for a description on how to use them with your dragon.

Clothing –

Your ritual, healing and spell work clothes should be comfortable and something you feel good about yourself in. I like to wear a T-shirt with airy yoga trousers or a long, breezy dress with my dragon amulet around my neck. If you feel you would like to have a special robe and headwear then that's entirely fine. I understand that more ornate clothing can lift a person out of the mundane and into a magickal frame of mind.

I personally like to keep things very simple and easy but we are all different and that's ok. It's great to have clothing that you only wear for your work with dragons. It helps give focus and your energy will switch into the right gear. It's a bit like putting on a uniform for work. You feel ready for that specific action and role.

Sacred Spaces & Altars

If you are able to give up an entire room specifically for your magickal work then you are lucky to be in an ideal situation, but if space is limited then you need to get creative. If, like me, you share your home with others who do not necessarily also share your need for an altar, then you can either adapt a small table or corner as your scared space or you can store your tools in a box or drawer and bring them out each time you use them. Whatever your situation, your sacred space will be as effective and beautiful as the effort you put into it. It's down to you to bring your energy and love to the area in which you work.

You will find that, over time, the area in which you work and the tools you use will begin to vibrate with the energy of your magick. The more positive your intentions are within your work, the more positive the vibration will be.

For Hearth Dragon witchcraft, it's very important to understand that your ultimate goal is to produce a beautiful harmony in your home that will impact the world beyond.

The work you do with your dragon will create energy that spirals into the universe, lights up your aura, can heal and restore balance, and leaves a residual magick in your home and community. Make sure this magick is created from love and compassion. You are responsible for the consequences of everything you do.

When you work with dragons, spirit guides and with love itself, you, your home and your family will benefit from the warmth and beauty that become tangible in your surroundings and in your mind.

Your home should be an extension of your sacred space. In Chapter 6, I will talk more about hearth-care and making your environment a place of nourishment and nurture.

ALTAR SET UP

Once you have found a location for your sacred space, you can assemble your working altar with all the items you have found, made or bought.

It is customary to place the five items that represent the five elements in accordance with their compass direction. This tends to differ slightly, according to culture and discipline. You need to do what feels right to you. For my own altar, I like to place the element of spirit (the dragon image) centrally, towards the back of the altar. I place an offering bowl in front of it. This is situated in the north. I place crystals around the dragon to represent earth (you can find a list of relevant crystals and uses in Chapter 7).

The tea light candles representing fire sit in the south. To the east I place the incense, representing air; and to the west are items representing water.

All of this resides on a tray on my coffee table in the living room, which I can move with ease to clean and rehome, if necessary, should the coffee table be required for mundane use (normally a spread of takeaway meals at the weekend and a bottle of wine!).

Keep the altar space and your tools clean and tidy. It's a sacred space and should be respected and maintained as such. Your working tools should be stored safely and out of the way of visitors and curious family members. The vibration of these tools will change should other people handle them.

Before doing any magickal work it is always best to do a purification chant to dispel any negative influence that your tools, your space, and you may have absorbed. This will be explained later in the Chapter.

YOUR CIRCLE

When I talk of the Circle, I can mean both the contained area in which you work and the people and astral helpers within it.

A bit like a 'circle of friends' or a Coven, your Circle will include you, your dragons, your spirit helpers and any other person(s) that works with you.

The cast Circle is the energetic circumference surrounding and protecting your area of work. It is this energetic boundary that we will now be discussing.

I don't want to fill you with any anxiety, but the truth is that if we are prepared to acknowledge the existence of dragons and spirit guides then we must accept that there are other beings and dimensions out there that we don't want to invite into our homes.

I have only once experienced the presence of something that wasn't very pleasant. It made me feel rather ill and compressed. I had watched a documentary on the TV about this particular type of entity. The programme was fascinating but halfway through it I began to feel very unwell and depressed and I could feel an unusual, gloomy pressure in the air. I turned the programme off and called in my guides who removed it immediately. I used the purification chant throughout my house for several consecutive days, to be on the safe side, and I'm glad to say it has never returned.

Be cautious about what you watch and read and open yourself to. Even if you have an insatiable appetite for learning, sometimes it's best to realise there are things that are better not to study in too much depth.

There has to be light and dark in order to bring balance. But your darkness should be filled with healing and wisdom and your light should always guide your direction.

Dragons are also full of light and darkness, guidance, wisdom and healing. They are not to be trifled with. They deserve respect and wonder. If you start to make demands of them or behave in a way that lacks integrity and kindness, they will not be happy. They will not harm you, but they will just bugger off and leave you to it.

Your Circle is sacred. It is a place for blending energies with those you trust and is therefore an energetic extension of the combined spirits of you and your team.

OPENING AND SEALING THE CIRCLE

Your working Circle may be an entire room, or it may be a small space at a table. You may wish to work seated or standing, depending on the amount of mobility and space you have.

Either way, the fundamentals of opening and sealing the Circle prior to your magickal work are the same. 'Opening the Circle' is the same as 'casting the Circle'. I use the term 'opening' as it's the direct antithesis of 'closing the Circle' and so it makes more sense to me to call it this.

For this task, you may wish to use your hand, your wand or your dagger/sword if that feels good to you and you have been instructed by others to use it. It doesn't really matter what you use, as long as you are focused and sincere in your intention.

Your intention here is to create an energetic boundary around your working area that seals the Circle to every being and energy except those whom you are inviting. The boundary Circle protects you and your team of friends, physical and astral.

... when you have:

- cleansed your sacred space,
- prepared your post-ritual refreshments,
- set up your altar and your tools,

- added a suitable offering for your dragons,
- had your ritual shower or bath,
- changed into your dragon work clothing,
- turned on your energy-boosting music,
- lit your candles and your incense,
- and ensured that you will not be disrupted by devices and people
- … then you are ready to begin.

Either walk around your altar, if you have room or, from a stationary position, move your hand around you. Using your chosen tool or fingers, move in a clockwise direction and draw a wide circle to encompass the whole area in which you are working. Imagine a bright streak of white fire blasting from your chosen tool or fingertip as it draws and seals the Circle around you.

As you do this, you can sing or chant this opening prayer. Feel free to create your own. If you do so, then be sure to include invitations of aid and protection from your spirit guides, your dragon helpers, the elements and the four directions.

Opening Prayer

This Circle is sealed,
In love and in light.
We call on the dragons,
Your power and might.

Teach us your wisdom,
Your courage and sight.

Protect us and aid us,
This ...... moon night (add the moon phase here).

We call on the spirits,
Our Guides, who with love.
Protect all around us,
Below and above.

We call the four quarters,
Unite us as One.
And Grandmother moon,
And Grandfather sun.

The Earth, the Air,
the Fire, the Water.
Come bring your power,
To aid our prayer.

After the Circle is opened and sealed, you are free to perform your ritual, healing or manifestation spell.

CLOSING THE CIRCLE

When finished, you must do the reverse. Walk or point with your chosen tool or hand and move anticlockwise around the altar, imagining the seal of light dissolving. Chant or sing the Closing Prayer as you do this.

As with the opening prayer you are encouraged to write your own closing prayer or use this one. If you write your own, then include thanks and farewell to the dragons, your spirit guides and the elements. Doing so will cause them to leave. You don't want any of these energies to be lingering around too close while you try to get on with your daily life.

Closing Prayer

We close this Circle,
We say farewell.
With thanks to the dragons,
And spirits as well.
We offer this gift (your offering),
And ask if you may,
Afford us protection,
Each night and each day.

The Earth, the Air,
The Fire, the Water,
Return, release, return again.

The Earth, the Air,
The Fire, the Water,
Return, release, return again.

After the completion of your prayer, you can indulge in your snack and drink and record what you have experienced and learnt in your magickal journal.

PURIFICATION

It is best to do a purification of your tools and space each time you work with them, and especially when you bring any new items into your home.

I like to do this in a very simple way once I've set up the altar by tinging my Tibetan bells 3 times. Once to purify all the tools on my altar, once for the room space, and once for me and anyone who is with me.

The healing and cleansing vibration of sound reaches every dark corner and nook and cranny without having to waft anything around, so I prefer this to other methods. You can also use smoke from incense, passing the objects through it and then moving it around the room and yourself. Or you can use saltwater to wash everything (except don't use this on metal, as it will be corrosive).

Whichever method you choose, you can chant these words while you do it:

Purification Chant

I cleanse and purify these tools so that they may be fit to serve me in my work.

I cleanse and purify myself so that I may channel positive energy in my work.

I cleanse and purify this space of all harmful, negative energy.

I bless this space, these tools and myself, with love, harmony and well-being.

Once you've done this, you can leave the object in full moonlight or in a sunny place so that it gets charged with the respective energy. Moonlight gives a watery energy and the sun gives a fiery energy, so choose which best suits your purpose.

DRAGON PROTECTION AMULETS

Dragons are great protectors and they can be invited to imbue an object with protection energy. Your object can be anything at all. My amulet is a silver dragon pendant that I wear around my neck that includes a turquoise stone which is my birthstone. Your amulet could be jewellery, or a statue, a mirror, a piece of clothing - literally anything can be used as an amulet.

Amulets repel negative energy.

It's best to do this protection spell in a formal way by getting yourself ready and prepared for ritual work as described previously.

CREATING AN AMULET

Intention: Create a protection amulet from an everyday object.
Moon Phase: Full or waning moon.

You will need:
- Prepared altar and sacred space.
- Bookmark the purification chant in Chapter 2 so you can find it easily.
- Chosen amulet object.
- Crystals: Black Tourmaline, Serpentine.

➢ **Open your Circle in the usual way.**

➢ **The Ritual**
- Purify yourself, your space and your tools, including the object to be used as an amulet, by using the

Purification process with sound, water or smoke and the chant in Chapter 2.

- Lay your black tourmaline and serpentine stones next to your amulet object on your altar and invite their protective energy to aid your intent.
- Then invite the dragons to help you by using these words:

> Dragons of land and sea and sky,
> Of earth and rivers come swim or fly.
> I ask for your protective might,
> Imbue this object with your light.
> Amulet repel all harm from me,
> From negative forces I am free.

- Point your wand at the object and let the energy flow through you and your wand and into the amulet. When you feel the energy flow diminish, put your wand down and hold the amulet in your hands. Feel the vibration of the object and know that it is ready.

➢ **Close your Circle in the usual way.**

➢ **Eat and drink your refreshments to help ground yourself.**

Like batteries, the amulet will need recharging periodically. How often you do this is up to you. You will know when it is necessary to do so, or your dragon may inform you.

You can recharge this amulet by placing it in sunshine or under a full moon or by placing a selenite crystal over it. Make your intention known. The energy will activate this way. The protection intent has already been placed on the amulet so there's no need to go through the whole ritual again.

WISDOM AND AWAKENING RITUAL

This is a kind of initiation and a request for guidance on any new path. This ritual is a kind of tool to give you a good start in your magickal journey with dragons.

It's a lovely ritual that leaves you feeling refreshed and reborn.

Intention: Initiation on your magickal path with dragons.
Moon Phase: New or full moon.

You will need:

- Your prepared altar space.
- Your magickal journal and pen.
- Oils & Teas: Dragon Wing Tea.
- Hearth Dragon Meditation Oil (see recipes in Chapter 10).

Prepare yourself, your altar and your room, put an offering in your offering bowl, make your tea, place the cup next to your altar, light your oil burner, add 3 drops of Hearth Dragon Meditation Oil and top up the burner dish with water. While you do this, know for sure that the tea and the scented oil are going to awaken and refresh your mind and heart.

➢ **Say or sing the Hearth Dragons Creed.**

➢ **Open your Circle in the usual way.**

➢ **The Ritual**

Sit comfortably with your tea, journal and pen close by and say:

> Dragons of wisdom I ask you to aid me on my journey of discovery,
> Guide me and teach me all I need to know.
> May I apply this knowledge in the pursuit of creative positive changes,
> For myself, my hearth and the community.

Take a sip of your tea and say:

> I drink this tea to heal from old scars and notions that may hinder my learning.
> I drink this tea to open my heart and mind to the wisdom of love and compassion.
> I free myself from old ways and thoughts that no longer serve me.
> I drink this tea so I can fly with dragons.

Now sit silently and let your thoughts drift. You may feel lightheaded because of the tea and dragon energy. This is fine and will help your connection, but bring your attention to the earth below you and send out some roots to anchor your spirit. You need to remain focused and clear-headed. You should feel happily balanced between earth and the astral level. I call it the 'Inbetweens'.

Allow the dragons to bring knowledge, guidance and ideas. If you are alert enough to do so, scribble them down in your magickal journal as they come.

Spend as long as you like doing this then bring yourself back to earth fully and slowly. Wriggle your fingers and toes, stretch, yawn and take invigorating breaths.

➢ **Close your Circle in the usual way.**

➢ **Eat and drink your refreshments to help ground yourself.**

➢ **Ponder and write all your new wisdom in your magickal journal.**

This is such a beautiful way to get to know your dragons and allow them to speak freely and help you. It clears the flight path for your important work ahead.

CHAPTER 4

Shadow Work

YOUR SHADOW SELF

'Know Thyself.' – From the Delphic Temple of Apollo, in Greece.

We are all light and dark with bits of grey and splatters of colour.

If you were a famous painting, what would you be? A riot of haphazard colour as in a Jackson Pollock or a calm, enigmatic 'Mona Lisa'? Maybe you are more straight lines and block colour like a Mondrian or a soft, blurry Monet.

Somewhere, at some point in your life, you are likely to have been 'The Scream' by Edvard Munch.

We are all a canvas of ever-changing lines and colour. Layer upon layer of experience and emotion has created who we are.

In order to work effectively with dragons, or any kind of magick, we need to find clarity within ourselves.

This means getting to know yourself and finding peace with who you are. In magick, we are working as channels of energy. Any blockages will result in disharmonious outcomes or perhaps no outcome at all.

Through shadow work, we can shine a light on the aspects of ourselves that we keep hidden in darkness. Once we have faced our shadows and acknowledged them, they can no longer pop up and surprise us. To this effect, they can no longer cause us harm.

I have heard people talk of the integration of the shadow self. When we integrate shadows as accepted parts of ourselves, they can be used as positives in our lives. They complete us. We can grow and learn and use our darker aspects to keep balance and a view and perspective of the world that is unique to us. It can help us navigate tricky roads and offer advice to others. We need the shadows. If we can get past the pain, hurt, guilt, grief and all the other emotions that come with it, we can find that at its source is wisdom.

Shadow work is a vast and in-depth journey of self-discovery which can be liberating but often painful. This Chapter only briefly introduces you to this kind of work and I encourage you to read the wonderful and helpful books out there by experts in the field and to learn more.

DRAGON ISLAND MIRROR MEDITATION

Before you embark on any shadow work, you need to be able to ground yourself, calm your mind and recall a feeling of safety.

It helps to have a grounding tool that can be held in your hands to remind you of all these things. In this meditation, you will hold a compact mirror, or a small mirror with a case, in your hands while you go on a journey to your dragon's place of safety and love. While you are there, you will fill the mirror with these feelings of love and safety and so turn your mirror into a talisman that can be used, held and focused upon whenever you feel a little wobbly and over-emotional. It will help to ground and rebalance you.

For this meditation you will need:

- A small compact mirror or a mirror with a case.
- Comfortable clothing to wear.
- A comfortable place to rest where you will not be disturbed.
- A cup of Dragon Wing Tea.

A JOURNEY TO YOUR DRAGON ISLAND

Hold your mirror in your lap while you sit comfortably. Breathe deeply and slowly and focus on your breath. Feel the air filling your stomach and allow it to expand and retract with no effort. Feel the air rushing up your nostrils and into your head, feel it filling your lungs. As you exhale release any tension in your body, your limbs, your hands. Loosen your jaw and your brow. Let your mouth be soft.

Just breathe. Just be. For a few minutes.

Now think about your dragon guide. Your friend and companion in your magickal work. Think about its eyes, its nostrils, its colour, skin and scales. Does it have wings? Is it long and sinewy, or stocky and strong? Do you know its name? If so call it now by its name, or simply call it your 'Dragon Guide'. Ask your dragon to join you on a journey to a beautiful place that you can share and that you can both feel safe within.

You are going to your own personal place of refuge, Dragon Island.

You find yourself on your dragon's back and holding on tightly as your mighty guide takes off into the air. Colours around you spin and sparkle. You fly up and out of your house feeling the cool rush of air on your face and limbs. You feel no fear, only exhilaration and freedom.

As the colours around start to fade and disperse you look down to see a stretch of turquoise sea glinting in the sunlight. Your dragon flies low to the surface of the small waves as they break and scatter white foam. Silver and crimson fish swim in shoals and turtles surface to take a look at you as your dragon's great shadow passes over the water.

You see ahead a stretch of white sand and an island of tropical plants and trees, a rainforest that circles a central mountain. The mountain rises high into the blue sky. Its top is ringed with clouds and the glint of white snow can be seen at its very peak. This mountain, this island belongs to you and your dragon. No other human can visit this place unless you have invited them. You hear the soft call of birds and mammals that live within the trees.

Your dragon lands heavily but expertly on the soft sand and crouches for you to slide from its back. Your feet are bare. The sand is warm and soft between your toes. The mirror is still in your hand. You check out your clothes. What are you wearing? You feel at this moment that you are allowed to just be you. You are your true magickal self.

The sea is clear, calm and inviting. A warm breeze greets you as you both head across the sand towards the forest and the mountain. Around you, boulders streaked with glittering veins of pink and green ore are scattered like giant marbles.

A low wooden house comes into view. It is painted white with blue shutters and a roof made of vast palm leaves. It is surrounded by plants and bright flowers, some that you have never seen before. So many colours and wonderful smells meet your senses. The blue door of the house is open and a curved path edged with pebbles leads to its threshold. Your dragon lies down and stretches out amidst sand and plants. With a snort and a shuffle, it makes itself comfortable while you enter the house.

The place is furnished simply. It is clean and cosy. A stone fireplace is already set with logs. Comfortable chairs look out at the view of the sea through the largest window. The bookcase is full of your favourite books and the table is set with your favourite food and drink. Candle lanterns hang ready to be lit at nightfall.

A bed, within an arched nook, stretches across the rear wall of the house and is soft with warm blankets and pillows.

Shells decorate the window sills and rugs soften the flagstone floor. A wind-chime of shells tinkles softly by the door as the sea breeze fills the little house with its cleansing, salty breath.

You sit yourself in one of the large chairs beside the hearth. In your lap, your small mirror can be felt. Hold it in your hand and bring it to your heart.

This Island and this house are your special retreat. Your cosy home that you and your dragon can return to at any time. You are safe here. You think of a name for your little beach house and imagine a wooden sign with the name painted on it, hanging outside by the door.

Now bring your mirror to your mouth and press your lips upon it. Breathe the name of your house and your contentment into your mirror. Know that every time you hold this mirror you hold the love, joy and safety of this island and this little house.

You can stay and rest in or explore your little house for as long as you want to.

When you are ready, rise and step into the doorway, taking in the view of the sunlit water and the bright sand and palm trees. Your dragon rolls happily in the sunshine, spraying sand over its scales and humming a song like the rolling of waves. You see your house's name sign hanging beside the door, just as you pictured it. Here, you can create your own perfect place to be.

You can stay on Dragon Island as long as you wish. You can explore the island and its treasures. The dense rainforest or the crystal cave in the mountain behind the waterfall. The river of sweet drinking water and the carved steps that ascend the mountain. They twist and turn around carvings of dragons and other creatures.

The choice is yours. Wherever you go your experience will be one of happiness and wonder and your dragon will be with you, looking after you and enjoying the time you spend together.

When you are ready to leave the island, your dragon will allow you upon its back once more.

It raises its snout into the air and lifts you both into the sky and up beyond into the swirling colours.

You grip your mirror in your hand as you leave and in a sparkle of lights and stars, you land back inside your usual home. Back again in the seating place you started in. Back in your room at home. Safe and well and refreshed. You breathe out a happy sigh and although you have experienced a useful and pleasant journey you are pleased to be home. You wiggle your toes and feel the ground again beneath your feet.

Your dragon is so happy to have made this journey with you. You can both return to this Island any time you like to explore the island or simply fly free above the ocean and over the mountains and clouds.

For now, your dragon bids you farewell and leaves you to your thoughts.

Now look at your small mirror. Hold it to your heart again and feel the joyous energy within it. It retains the energy of that beautiful island, your little house and your dragon's love. It also holds within it the freedom and safety of your island home, the cleansing of the sea and the sea breeze, and the grounding energy of the feel of soft, warm sand between your toes.

This mirror is now your talisman of safety and contentment as well as your tool for learning about yourself.

MIRROR EXERCISE – THE SHADOW & THE LOOKING GLASS

You will need:
- Your magickal journal.
- Your talisman compact mirror – or talisman small mirror with a case.
- A comfortable, distraction-free space in which to work.

Shadows can be gossamer and fleeting and they can be dark and seemingly endless.

Your shadows, in whatever capacity, are always of your own making. No one, no situation, can make the shadows for you … they can contribute to the emotions involved in creation, but your shadow is created by you.

This means, that it can also be rewritten, recreated and even erased by you, its sole artist and author.

Your little mirror is a talisman of safety when shut or in its case. Open it now and see your own reflection. Now the mirror is your useful tool.

You can close it again any time you like and feel the energy of safety once more. You can revisit your retreat on Dragon Island and return when you feel ready.

For now, look at your face. Look at your skin, its colours and textures. Your nose and nostrils as they breathe and your mouth as it lifts into a slight smile and then into a pout.

Some of you will find it uncomfortable to scrutinise your own face and others will enjoy the view. Wherever you are with your self-image know that this face is part of you. It is unique and expressive and it served you well your whole life so far. It laughs with you, cries with you and moves with every emotion.

Look into your eyes. Look at the flecks of light and colour.

What do your eyes tell you today?

- Have you had enough sleep?
- Are you taking good care of yourself?
- Are you eating well and drinking enough water?

Look deeper into your eyes.
- What story do they hold of today? What can they tell you about today?
- What can they tell you about yesterday?
- What can they tell you about last week? Last month? Last year?

- What stories do they hold about your life so far?
- What comes to mind when you think about your life's stories?
- How would you summarise your life if it was a book?
- What would it look like if it was a triptych of paintings? Past, present and future.

As you look into your eyes tell yourself what you like about yourself, tell yourself what you dislike about yourself.

- Why do you dislike this aspect of yourself?
- What else do you dislike?
- Are there parts of your life that you are not content with?
- Can you change them?
- If so, how?
- If not, can you accept them or change your view of them?

- What makes you angry?
- Why?
- What makes you happy?
- Why?

Think of all the people your eyes have seen

- Who are the people that spring easily to mind?
- How do you feel about them?
- How do you think they feel about you?
- When you think about these people do your eyes change?

- When you think about yourself what happens to your eyes?
- What do you see?

- Do you need to find forgiveness?
- Who do you need to forgive?
- Can you find forgiveness?
- For others?
- For yourself?

- What now needs to be released from your life?
- How will this release affect you?
- What can be gained from this release?

And most importantly your eyes will tell you …
- What wisdom have your shadows taught you?

Look into your eyes and know that there is wisdom.
- That all the shadows of your past have brought wisdom.
- Smile and thank the shadows for all the learning it has bestowed and the experiences that have made you into a unique and thoughtful human being.
- Feel gratitude for the shadows, even the painful ones, for they are the ones that have taught you most of all.
- Be honest with yourself about the answers to these questions. Take your time with each one.
- If at any time you feel overwhelmed or uncomfortable just close the mirror, hold it in your hands and

let the energy of the sea breeze refresh you and the little house comfort and contain you. Feel the warm sand under your feet and between your toes. Breathe and relax.

- Feel the breath of your friend and guide, your dragon, as it draws near and will stay with you as long as you need it.

- Now close your eyes and let the thoughts, memories and experiences come and go.
- Breathe deeply and slowly and know that you have made a good start in getting to know your own shadow.
- No one said this was going to be easy. If you feel very overwhelmed with this exercise then leave it alone. It may help to see a therapist. As I said before, we are just touching the basics here as an introduction. We all have shadows but if yours are painful to the point of not being able to confront them at all then you should consider help from a professional therapist before you ever embark on any kind of magickal work at all.
- We all have a responsibility for our own mental and physical health and sometimes we all need a bit of help.

- Now get yourself a cup of your favourite tea or coffee and eat a tasty snack.
- Congratulate yourself on your courage and your honesty with yourself.

- In your journal, you can write down anything that seemed particularly important or surprising about your looking glass exercise.
- Write down any areas that you feel you need to work on yourself or could get expert help with from a therapist.
- Write down also the notions of wisdom that you have learnt.

Writing things down can help to normalise thoughts that you have repressed and bring them into the light.

Shadow areas to think about:
- What do you need to accept?
- What do you need to change?
- What do you need to release?
- What areas require greater courage for you to deal with them?

In the next section, you will find simple and easy rituals to help manifest energy for each of these areas.

In Chapter 5, you will find Forgiveness & Healing and Showers & Baths.

For each of the below rituals you will need to prepare yourself, your refreshments, your tools, and your sacred space and use the instructions and prayers/chants as discussed in Chapter 3.

DRAGON FIRE & SMOKE RELEASE RITUAL

Intention: Release of that which no longer serves you.

Moon Phase: Waning moon.

You will need:
- Prepared altar space (inside or outside) – be mindful of fire safety.
- A small cauldron or fireproof bowl.
- A charcoal disc.
- Strips of paper.
- A pen.
- Silver birch leaves or twigs (optional, but help with the energy of release).

➢ **Open your Circle in the usual way.**

➢ **The Ritual**
- Give yourself a few minutes to clarify in your mind what it is that needs releasing and why.
- Decide how you are going to action this in your daily life. What needs to be done, or not done, in order to achieve the intended release?
- Ask your dragon guide(s) to help you find wisdom and clarity on this subject. Listen to anything they have to say and be open to any signs and feelings they may manifest for you.
- When you are sure you have come to a conclusion that releasing will be a healthy option for you,

without harming anyone else, then write down the thing(s) to be released on a strip of paper.

- Light the charcoal inside the fireproof bowl and wait for it to glow orange and then become white with ash.
- Place the silver birch leaf/twig and strip of paper with the writing on the charcoal and as it burns say:

> With dragon fire, I burn to dust,
> That which wisdom deems I must.
> No longer keep or need to know
> With dragon smoke, I let it go.

Watch it smoke and disappear into the air (if you are indoors then make sure your windows are open and ensure the flames cannot catch anything alight around it). Watch the smoke float with your thing to release, into the sky, never to return.

Now see and feel your life without this thing/person that no longer serves. How has your life improved? How do you move forward from this day?

➢ **Close your Circle in the usual way.**

➢ **Eat and drink your refreshments to help ground yourself.**

DRAGON WATER ACCEPTANCE RITUAL

Intention: To accept that which cannot be changed.

Moon Phase: Dark or waning moon.

You will need:
- Prepared altar space.
- Bowl of filtered or spring water - Ensure the bowl is wide enough to place your hands in.
- Hearth Dragon Meditation Oil (see Chapter 10 for recipe)
- Clean towel for drying hands and face.
- White candle.

➢ **Open your Circle in the usual way.**

➢ **The Ritual**
- Light the white candle and ponder on the subject that requires acceptance.
- Let any negative feelings come and go. If fear is a predominant feeling, then also include the courage chant below in this ritual.

If you know in your heart that nothing can be changed and that you need to move forward and cope with whatever is, what has been, and what may come, then ask your dragons to help you find peace with this decision.

Add a couple of drops of the Hearth Dragon's Oil to the water and say:

Dragons of water give courage and healing.
Give strength to my heart to accept what I'm feeling.
Give patience, compassion and determination,
To accept with good grace, this situation.

- Now wash your hands and face in the water and wash away fear and doubt.
- Dry yourself with the clean towel and know that you are cleared of negative emotions.
- Have faith that whatever comes, even if it is painful, is necessary for the bigger plan.
- The wheel of life keeps turning.
- Nothing is forever, except, when it is pure, Love.

➢ **Close your Circle in the usual way.**

➢ **Eat and drink your refreshments to help ground yourself.**

DRAGON ENERGY COURAGE CHANT

- Light a candle, and let thoughts of whatever you need courage for come and go in your mind. Imagine yourself dealing with this situation. Imagine yourself feeling strong and knowing that because you are strong you are more able to help others going through the same fear.
- There is no courage without fear and the fact that you are facing this with honesty means you are already brave.

- Call in your dragons and feel their might and power. It flows through you and will remain with you for as long as you need. This kind of power and strength can lay dormant inside you and then spread its wings and carry you high when you most need it. It is always inside you.
- Take deep breaths, hold your head high, your back straight, shoulders back and focus on the flame of the candle.
- Say this chant:

> As this flame burns bright before me,
> So, my heart grows ever-strong.
> Dragon courage burns within me,
> Their strength and fire reside for long.
>
> I am ready for my challenge
> My mind is wise, my heart set free.
> We are ready for the challenge
> My dragon and the warrior me.

- Now know that you are not alone. You have support and guidance and as long as you take your own action to help yourself and others, you will always have dragon wings to bear some of the weight.

CHAPTER 5

Magick in the Mundane – Self-care

There's been a big surge of self-care guidance and products available lately. Of all the fashions and fads that emerge in today's society, I feel this one is one of the good ones. Never before have we been made so aware of the need to take care of ourselves. Our diet, our water intake, our sleep patterns, physical exercise, stress-management, are just a few that have come to light.

For a lifestyle that involves witchcraft of any kind, maintaining physical, mental and spiritual health is of great importance.

You need a lifestyle that encourages simplicity and self-love. If you are wading through your own complicated, busy, stress-filled and less-than-nourishing routine on a daily basis, how are you going to be able to channel pure dragon energy or elemental and celestial energy, and how are you going to have the clarity and focus required to help other people, your family, friends, community, the world?

To be well-balanced and effective witches, wizards, magicians and healers of the Earth, we need to take back as much control as possible over our lives. We can't control everything. There are circumstances and situations and health issues that happen to us without invitation. We can, however, control how we cope with these occurrences and we can control how we nourish our lives and that of our dependant families, in order to be best able to find strength and clarity when needed.

When I talk about nourishment here, I don't just mean food. Nourishment also comes from friendships, rewarding jobs, a happy family and harmonious home, clean and tidy surroundings, personal hygiene, getting outside into nature, and all the other things that make your life rich and enjoyable and bring the benefit of good physical and mental health.

For people like ourselves, who are aware of how the use and manipulation of energy can change things for the better, there are many ways witchcraft can aid us in creating a more nourishing life.

Included here are just a few that you can incorporate into your day.

HEALING WATER

Water is often taken for granted in Western society. It is provided on tap, in bottles and falls out of the sky. It is cyclical and forever. Despite it being a common element, especially in the British Isles where rain is the normal state of play, water is still providing us with many surprising qualities, as the research of scientists like Veda Austin can testify. Water has been proven to have memory and a conscious state that is able to 'listen' and communicate through changing crystal structure.

With this in mind, it is therefore sensible to assume that we can communicate with water, both inside our bodies and also outside. We can, in fact, request a change in the structure of the water to facilitate our needs.

You can talk to the water inside your own body and request it to heal you.

You can do this simply by just asking, or you can use a chant like the one below:

> Water, water, inside me,
> Set your healing crystals free.
> Give me life and give me strength,
> Give me lots of energy.

Take note when you use it of any changes you can feel in your body. I've very often felt the soft vibration like tiny bubbles in my veins, followed by a rejuvenation of my energy levels and a lightening of my mood.

HEALING SHOWERS & BATHS

Showers and baths are an excellent way to give yourself a little self-care. Not only are they providing your personal hygiene needs but also, they are a time for solitude and reflection and healing. Baths and showers can ease a troubled mind and aching body. The warm water, sweetly fragrant soaps, purifying bath salts and the addition of herbs and blessings can turn a mundane task into the most sacred and beneficial ritual that can be enjoyed every day.

Stand under the shower and let the surge of warm water purge your face and body of tension. Let it wash the cares and woes of your spirit down the plug hole. Even if you have to reclaim them again in order to deal with life, for now, give yourself this moment to just be. Enjoy the sensation of the clean water and soap. Cleanse yourself with a fragrant lather and as you rinse the grime away, say:

Heal my skin, and all within.

This is nice and short and easy to remember and you can use it as often as you need.

My husband, who is quite the joker ... sigh ... has his own version:

Soap and water, do what you aughta ...

I did have to laugh when he recited this to me. Although I didn't laugh quite as much as he did ... but I guarantee his version is the one you will remember! This is fine, just make sure your intent is clear in your mind or the water won't know what it aughta …

PREPARING YOURSELF FOR MAGICKAL WORK – BATH OR SHOWER PURIFICATION

Having a ritual bath or shower before you perform any kind of magick is a lovely way to prepare yourself as a conduit for the energy needed. I suggest having a special soap for this task if using the shower or adding the Dragon Wing Tea infusion (found in Chapter 10) to a bath.

Whether using an herbal soap or adding the tea, make clear your ritual intent as you do so.

You can use this chant:

Purifying Bath and Shower Chant
These herbs so sweet and water kind,
Cleanse and purify my body and mind.
Lift my vibration, and focus my sight,
To channel my dragons in love and in light.

Furthering the shadow work discussed in the previous Chapter, if, while you were searching your shadow, you found that there were people or situations that you need to disentangle yourself from emotionally, then a cord-cutting bath can be very useful.

When you are 'cutting cords', you are not banishing anything or anyone from your life, you are just getting rid of the overwhelming attachment that might be hindering your life choices. It's a way of setting yourself free of harmful emotions, whilst maintaining a healthy relationship.

It's a useful tool if there are people or situations in your life that you don't want to be without but need to rid yourself of associated negative emotional ties.

CORD CUTTING BATH

Intention: To cut the cords with emotions and situations that no longer serve you.

Moon Phase: Waning moon.

If you don't have a bath, then use the herb infusion to lather your usual soap whilst you are in the shower.

You will need:
- A warm bath/shower.
- A sprig of rosemary (or a few drops of rosemary essential oil).
- A spring of lemon balm (or a few drops of lemon balm essential oil).
- A handful of Himalayan bath salt.

- Make an infusion in a heat-proof jug or teapot by adding the rosemary and lemon balm to boiling water.
- Let it steep until the water is cool enough not to scold you when handled.

- Run your bath/shower and remove your clothing as you usually do when bathing, and any jewellery that is restrictive or uncomfortable. You want to feel liberated.
- Pour the salt and the infusion into your warm bath and get in. Relax. Enjoy the scent of the herbs. If you are showering, add a pinch of salt to your jug of infusion and use it to lather your soap. Start to wash yourself, think of the person or thing that you wish to cut cords from and, as you do so, say:

Cord Cutting Bath Chant

I call upon the energy of my dragon guide and the
    water dragons,
To help me find my own strength.
As water is both kind and powerful, so am I made of
    such duality.

May the water of this bath (shower) cleanse and heal
    me,
With rosemary, lemon balm and salt to purify &
    protect me.
I wash myself of all negative energy,
I cleanse myself of all harmful connections to …
May any guilt, hurt, need and harmful attachment to
    the past leave me,
As I cut cords and move forward (you can imagine
    physically cutting the cords if it helps).
May only love, respect, and compassion remain,
I stand independently. I live my own life. I stand in my
    own power.

- Now imagine yourself in the life that you have created. A life liberated from harmful emotional ties. You are free to enjoy the changes that you have now made.
- Feel the healing of the water and the calm and peace within your mind and body.

AFFIRMATIONS

Affirmations are positive mantras that condition the mind to create confidence in your own success.

You can create your own affirmation for any personal trait that you wish to affirm.

They can be short and non-specific. For example:

I am fabulous.
Or they can remind you of your own power …
I am the Dragon Rider!
They can assist in gaining your desires …
I have all that I need and all that I want.
Or they can be long and all-encompassing …

I am the Dragon Rider,
I am balanced in mind and body,
I am courageous and strong.

I am the Dragon Rider,
I am beauty and kindness,
I am wealthy and generous.

Whatever you decide, ensure that the wording is positive.

The subconscious mind cannot deal with a negative that explains a positive. It will only hear the negative and retain it.

- e.g. Instead of saying:

  I am not angry and opinionated.
- Say instead:

  I am serene and open-minded.

Self-belief and confidence are a necessary foundation for working with dragons. Affirmations can be very helpful in this.

FOOD AND DRINK – NOURISHMENT & BLESSINGS

I am not a dietician or a nutritionist, so I'm not going to tell you what to or what not to eat. There are plenty of very informative sources where you can gain insight into this according to your own health needs.

Instead, I want to talk about the need for the revival of what, when I was a child, was called 'Saying Grace'.

At school, we would say a prayer over our food to voice our gratitude for it. As a child, it was something I just used to mumble as quickly as possible, so that I could get on with eating my marmite sandwiches.

Now that I'm older than dust, I realise that being grateful for and blessing our food is a way to cast a beautiful spell over it and infuse it with beneficial energies for the health of myself and my family. With reference again to the conscious, changing state of water crystals, food and drink contain water. If we prepare our food with negative thoughts and words then we are sending negative instructions to the water content of the food, and ourselves.

We can't change how our food is produced and shipped, or how much piping and chemical treatment our water has to suffer before reaching our taps, but we do have control over how we prepare and serve it.

Have respect for the sacrificed life of both plants and animals. Have respect for our life-giving water. Spare a thought for all the labour and energy of the people who have helped your food grow and find its way to your table, and have gratitude for the nourishment it gives you and those with whom you share it. It's a basic kitchen and hearth-witch philosophy and one that also well-serves Hearth Dragon witchcraft.

Food and Drink Blessing

May this food and drink be blessed with love,
And gratitude,
May it serve as medicine to my/our needs.

GRATITUDE MEDITATION

You will have already come across some working meditations in this book. The meditation I want to speak of now, however, is of a different kind. The previous meditations were those that were done in order to connect with an outside energy.

A communication with dragons and a connecting to a safe place

The other kind of meditation is one where you simply just sit and be. An internal meditation as opposed to an external one. It's a time for you to allow your body to stop producing the stress-induced chemical, cortisol, and let your blood return to its normal state of health. It's a relaxation that will help you see the outside world with more clarity and perspective.

As within, so without. Whatever you are feeling on the inside will be mirrored by life on the outside.

I suggest that you do this kind of meditation at least once a day, for ten minutes if possible or as long as you can allow. But do it regularly. Your fight and flight mode needs to simmer down for a while.

You can do this in the bath, in bed at night or in the morning. You can do this in a garden, on the living room floor, on the toilet even ... just use whatever time you have that's free of interruption.

All you need to do is sit. Straighten your back and rest your hands on your knees or in your lap. Close your eyes, then breathe. Don't try to empty your mind. You won't. Thoughts will come. Let them, but keep bringing your mind back to now and the space you are in at the moment. If something pops into your head that worries you, tell yourself you will better cope with it after you have given yourself this time to heal.

All you need to do in your life is get on with your days, one at a time, the best you can. Tell yourself this. Keep breathing. At this moment you are resting, and this is as important as any action.

When you have given yourself some time to just be, open your eyes and think of three things that you are grateful for. Smile. Say thank you. Take a long deep breath and then get on with the rest of your day.

Exercise

This section is pretty obvious to everyone. Keep as active and as fit as you can. The amount of physical exercise you do will depend on circumstances and physical ability. Staying as healthy and as mobile as your body will allow will benefit your whole life and also your mental health.

Working with magick needs to be approached with a holistic view of lifestyle choices. Being kind to yourself and caring for yourself comes before anything else.

I'm no expert in physical fitness but I like to combine my own simple, daily yoga routine with the opening of the main energy points of the body. These are the chakras. They are related to your physical health, your mental health and your emotional health. They are also very important when working with dragons.

The Chakras

There is a sea of information relating to the chakras. I strongly advise you to do more research into them. If you are physically able, then you may find chakra yoga to be a useful tool in tuning your body for channelling dragon energy. Physical exercise is one way to unblock these spinning gateways of energy but you can also do this through chants and meditation.

Dragons are especially connected to your chakras because each one identifies with a specific colour. Dragons like to use colour in their communication with you and use colours symbolically to help explain things.

There is also the kundalini aspect of chakra work. Kundalini is the energy of the divine feminine that, when awakened, rises from the base of your spine and weaves like a serpent or dragon through all the chakras and emerges through the crown at the top of your head. The awakening of the kundalini is a spiritual term for the release of life energy, or prana, that may begin a path of enlightenment.

The kundalini dragon can be awakened in various ways – through yoga, meditation or because of a deeply emotional experience. It feels explosive, like a sneeze or an orgasm and there is an opinion that the energy is a highly condensed form of sexual energy.

I touch briefly upon the aspect of the chakras here, as I feel it has relevance, but it is a massive source of learning in its own right and anyone would benefit from more research into it.

For the purposes of our dragon magick, we can be content to ensure our chakras are working efficiently by eating healthy foods, keeping active (mentally and physically), reducing stress in our lives, getting enough sleep (so important!) and doing this meditation:

CHAKRA DRAGON MEDITATION

The Chakras, from top to bottom:

- 7 Crown – Purple/White – Clarity and Connecting with Spirit, Cosmic Dragon Energy.
- 6 Third Eye – Indigo – Intuition, Imagination, Air Dragon Visions.
- 5 Throat – Blue – Communication, Water Dragon Truths.
- 4 Heart – Green – Self-love, Earth Dragon Protection and Healing.
- 3 Solar Plexus – Gut-feelings, Water Dragon Courage.
- 2 Sacral – Orange – Sexual Energies, Passion, Fire Dragon Creativity.
- 1 Root – Red/Brown – Safety, Security, Earth Dragon Energy.

- Light a candle and ask your dragon guides for aid in balancing your chakras, so that you might become a better channel for their energy.

- Imagine your chakra points are opening lotus flowers.
- Work your way from root to crown visualising the colours of each chakra and the feelings and respective emotions that go with it. Imagine your root chakra at the base of your spine, glowing red and spinning and drawing up earth energy into your body. Let the energy snake upwards to

each chakra in turn. As you move to each chakra, imagine it spinning with its own colour at its point in your body. When you reach the crown, let the energy flow up into the sky and also back down again through your chakras, through your body and into the earth.

- You are part of a great, constant circle of energy that is revitalising every part of you.
- When you are ready to end the meditation, imagine your chakras closing up like coloured lotus flowers, but continuing to spin efficiently.
- Ask your dragons to step back and help you stay grounded, protected and balanced.

CONNECTING WITH NATURE

There is nothing as valuable to your mental health as spending time amidst trees and plants, near lakes or the sea, in a field, in a garden, a park, a moorland, a balcony, or just being aware of the sky from a window. However you choose to get your fix of outdoor energy, ensure that you do it as regularly as possible.

Connecting with nature has become a bit of a cliché, but when you really do feel that connection, the oneness with the natural world, it can teach you to keep your thoughts in balance and understand priorities.

Dragons are elemental creatures and any communication with earth, water and sky will improve your relationship with the mighty creatures and spirits that live within them. It will also help you connect with yourself – your true self. The self that is so much more expansive than your physical body. The self that doesn't just look at the clouds floating by, hear the wind in the leaves and know the feel of cool stream water through their fingers, but is part of it. Your true self is always connected to the natural world.

Everything is energy. There are no definable boundaries and edges to a world of vibration. Our energetic bodies are as much a part of the landscape as the trees, the water, and the wild creatures.

I have read books relating to the 'higher self', the 'magickal self', the 'divine self' and the 'spiritual self'. I wonder if they are all the same thing. Whatever you want to call it or however you feel you need to find it, there is no doubt in my mind that the true self is entirely present when it is blending and basking within a natural land and skyscape.

I also feel that dragons can be found blending and basking in nature. Like us, they are energy and can absorb it and create from it.

The next time you are outdoors in a place that makes your heart sing, call in your dragons and spirit guides to share this experience with you. Allow your energy body, your aura, to expand into the space around you. Let it roam freely. Feel it reaching into the ground below you and merging with the sky. Your dragons might wish to connect their energy with yours. You might find that you can feel your dragon's presence in your auric space and you may be given an insight into the wisdom of these creatures as their knowledge touches your face like sunlight and moonlight and brushes your skin like a breeze. Dragons can talk to you through the rippling of water, the dancing of leaves or the sweet scent of roses.

Close your eyes for a few moments, relax, and enjoy being nothing more, no more or less important than the tiny ant crossing your path.

JOURNALING

I have already touched upon the need to keep a magickal journal throughout your dragon witchcraft practice. If you choose to keep a personal, diary-type journal also then that's a great way to empty daily thoughts and happenings out of the mind and into the physical. Writing and drawing can bring emotions into the light. Having to explain an emotion on paper is a useful way of normalising and reducing it to a manageable size.

Your magickal journal is for recording your rituals, healing and spells with dragons, for noting any thoughts and ideas that spring from and for your energy work and for recording the outcome and consequences of your work. It is also for writing down any communication-based knowledge that you have been given by your dragon guides and any reflective thoughts these may have raised. Be sure to date your entries. It's really useful to be able to look back on your progress and find any synchronicities, recurring aspects and foreshadowing that may have occurred. It's valuable to learn from the outcomes of your energy work. You will begin to understand what works and what doesn't.

Your grimoire, book of shadows or spell book will keep a log of the working details of the work. What for, how, when and where? But your magickal journal will keep a record of the happenings, notions and emotions resulting from the work.

LUNAR PHASES – THE CYCLE OF ENERGY

Working in accordance with the phases of the moon will greatly enhance your work with dragons. Our bodies, like our planet, are comprised of 60–70% water. The same can be said for most other mammals. A greater percentage is found within reptiles and amphibians and also insects. Plants carry an even greater percentage of water.

The moon, as governor of the great tides of the sea also has an effect on the flora and fauna of our Earth. We have our ebb and flow. During a waning moon, our energy decreases and during a waxing moon, we start to feel more active. A dark moon can render us almost debilitated and tired but as soon as the new moon is born, we start to revive and regenerate. A full moon increases energy to capacity. It can make us feel restless and edgy but is also the most powerful time to do any energy work.

It is for this reason that living by the moon cycles can have a beneficial effect on our physical, emotional and mental well-being, as well as providing the correct energy for spell work and ritual. I keep a moon calendar in my daily planner, so that I am always aware of when the best time is to plan certain activities.

Waning Energy

On the days leading up to a dark moon, when the moon is waning, you don't want to plan to do anything too strenuous. It's not possible for many of us to change work timetables every month to accommodate this, but try to be kind to yourself during these weeks. Get as much rest and sleep as you can and eat nourishing food. Drink plenty of water and allow yourself to enjoy home-based luxuries in the evenings.

In terms of your work with dragons, the waning moon is a good time for any spell or ritual that has the intent to release or cast off something. The energy is gentle and is great for healing and reflection, for shadow work and acceptance. It's a time to forgive and take special care of yourself and others.

Spend some time at the dark moon talking to your dragon guide about things you need to get off your chest and things you need to change for the better.

It's also a good time for journeying and flying with your dragon or visiting your Dragon Island safe place.

Waxing Energy

The weeks after the new moon, as she waxes into fullness, are the best times to plan your new adventures. Your energy will be rising and new projects and ideas will be in full flight. It's a time of action.

Your dragon magick will benefit from this energy, should your intent be for success and abundance, fertility and new relationships, love, passion, inspiration, courage, new enterprises, confidence and strength.

Full Moon Energy

Whatever you do on a full moon, the energies will be amplified. It's a great time to do any spell work and rituals. Your dragon will be able to help you harness this beautiful energy. It's a lovely time for rituals involving singing and dancing.

You can also leave your tools out or on a window sill to be recharged in the full moon's light. You can make moon water to put in an energising bath or cleanse your altar with by leaving a jar of rain, filtered or spring water in the moonlight.

The full moon is a time of completion and is a good time to look back at what you have achieved during the waxing lunar month and what you might need to change or release during the waning phase to come. It's a time of gratitude and so is a good time to do your gratitude meditation.

It's also a good time to do spells that require a lot of energy. A huge new, long-term project or the go-getting of your lifelong dream will benefit from a blessing and success spell on this day.

On the full moon evening, if you have friends who share your dragon work, you can get together for a feast and collaborative celebration ritual. Enjoy the energy and seize the opportunity to create and build on the life you want to live.

CHAPTER 6

Magick in the Mundane – Hearth Care

Central to Hearth Dragon philosophy is care of the home. Now, I have to mention here that I'm no housework expert. My husband, in fact, is a much better housekeeper than I am but I do try very hard to keep our home cheery, clean and comfortable. I don't always achieve this. Our home is far from perfect and not at all Instagram-worthy. But I want it to be a lovely place to spend our time, and I'm aware of changes that are necessary and that means I'm halfway there.

Maintaining a lifestyle that you wish for yourself is a long-term, continual process in which there are good days and challenging days. The main thing is to climb back up and ride that dragon to Sweetsville even if you've just fallen off at Shitsville.

It's not always easy, juggling work, family commitments, social events, and appointments and maintaining a grip on the ever-growing laundry pile, cleaning schedule and home maintenance. Add to that the worries about loved ones, financial stress and health issues, and life becomes a crucible of tasks.

Actually finding the time, amidst all of this, for self-care and dragon magick can seem like an impossibility but, if you consider that care of your home, your hearth, is also self-care and also part of dragon magick, then you can begin to feel that you are making some headway into living the life you were meant for.

HEART IS IN THE HEARTH

Your home is your sanctuary. If you live with others, it is a shared sanctuary. It is your place of retreat after a busy day and the place in which your mental and physical health is nurtured and nourished. Your home should feel like a warm hug for everyone who lives there. A massive percentage of our income is spent on items for the home. We invest money, time and energy into our homes, and so it's only sensible that we also invest love into its maintenance.

Your hearth should be cherished. When you spend time cleaning it you can be pouring love into it. When you freshen up the paintwork, vacuum the floors, plump up the cushions, dust the tops, put the dishes away, clean the toilet, add fresh towels to the bathroom ... all the mundane tasks ... all these tasks can be acts of love. But if you are merely going through the motions of these tasks, or actively hating every minute of it, then you are effectively washing your home with negative energy. Your energy can either fill your home with positive vibes or it can create a sour, miserable atmosphere for everyone that lives there.

So next time you are cleaning the bath and your back aches and you just want to get it done quickly (yep, that's also me, every time), remember to at least feel proud of the fact that you are still making an effort despite the discomfort and you are doing so because you love your home and those who share it with you.

ROSEMARY AND LEMON CLEANING LIQUID

Another good way to infuse your home with positive energy is to make your own magickal cleaning liquid. This is very easy to do but does take a little forethought.

You just need a glass bottle with a spray trigger. You can buy them for about £3 online ... white vinegar, a lemon or orange and some sprigs of rosemary.

Peel the lemon or orange (use the fleshy part in a salad or sliced up in a drink). Put the peel into the glass bottle and half fill with white vinegar. Add the sprig of rosemary.

As you do this, ask your dragon guides to infuse it further still with their lovely protective energy for your home. The lemon will bring joy and invigoration and the rosemary will act as a mild disinfectant, dispel harmful energies and also help to protect your home.

Give it a good shake and leave it for two weeks to infuse.

After this time, top up the bottle with water, shake it again, and it's ready to use.

You can use it to clean anything that isn't varnished. At first, it smells a bit vinegary but this doesn't last long and will soon leave your home smelling very clean.

You can use a mantra as you clean:

> I rid my home of grime today,
> All negative energy washed away.
> With love and kindness, I replace,
> With joy and peace, I fill this space.

COLOUR AND DÉCOR

You don't need to spend a fortune to have an inviting home. Whatever your style and budget be aware of colour choices and how they affect your mood. Different colours will affect different people in different ways. Lighting also has a huge impact on how we feel. I don't fare well with bright electric lights. Soft lighting from lamps and candles helps me feel relaxed and cosy. Warm colours are better for my mental health than the more fashionable greys and neutrals, so I decorate accordingly. This may be the opposite for you. Be aware of how your surroundings make you feel and how they affect others sharing your home. Experiment with different colours in the room.

Your dragon magick will greatly benefit from a home that uplifts and nurtures you. Your dragons will be aware of the energies of the colours in the room and how they affect your own vibration.

SACRED SPACE

For work with dragons and opening/casting Circles in which to do spells and rituals, you will need a space that will accommodate your altar and yourself (and others that you might work with). This could be a permanent set up, or a space that doubles up as a dining table, or coffee table, bed, etc. Whatever space you are using, be sure to give it a good clean before you start, both energetically and physically and then set up your area so that it feels good, smells good and looks like it will inspire magick. Use lighting, incense and music to bring the required atmosphere and energy to your sacred space. Treat it with respect and reverence. This space, for the duration of your ritual, will host dragons, spirits and elementals. You may not see them, but if you invite them, I promise, they will be there.

HOME VIBRATIONS – SHARED SPACES

Be aware that every person who enters your home ... you, your family ... your friends ... the neighbours ... the meter-reader ... the grocery delivery person ... everyone will bring their own energies into your hearth. Not all of these energies will be positive and most will linger for varying degrees of time.

Use your little bells, your cleaning routine, or your incense to regularly clear the vibrations from your home.

You can use the purification chant in Chapter 3 as you do this.

GARDENS & INDOOR PLANTS

If you are working with any kind of elemental witchcraft it's beneficial to have plants around you.

If you have a garden then you can set up an outdoor altar space, if you don't have a garden then you can add plants to your indoor space. Wherever you have your green space it's also good to include a water feature of some kind (this can be as simple as a small bowl of rainwater) some wind-chimes to represent air and a candle holder for your fire element. You can add stones and crystals and shells and make sure you have a comfortable place to sit and enjoy it all.

Plants add their own energy to any space and if they are well-tended, they will always bring healing and peace to your heart. You could add plants that you can also use in your magick. Herbs are often aromatic, beautiful and useful. You can use them in your food and your spells. I keep a pot of basil on my kitchen windowsill in summer and it serves as both a culinary herb (wonderful with tomatoes, mozzarella and olive oil) and also as a source of prosperity energy for my home. It smells wonderful and gives a splash of lovely fresh green to the room.

Keeping plants indoors will keep your air clean and your mind clear.

You can also train yourself to feel the energy of plants. Ask your dragons to help you tune in to the healing energies of any plants around you and you will be amazed at how light-headed you can become with the vibration.

I first learnt about the healing energy of plants from my dog, Riley, who, after his knee operation, would stand under a particular plant in my garden, called Tiger Grass, and he would quiver. As I approached him, I felt a powerful energy emanating from the plant. I felt drunk on the vibration and I noticed that my dog also had the same glazed look in his eye. I realised at this point that he had activated a healing energy from the plant from his own need. There was an unspoken communication between dog and plant and the plant had responded to his need for healing.

For me, this was the start of my journey into earth magick, which then led me to communication with beings and dragons that were protecting the Earth. My dogs have always been my teachers, and they too, like other animals, have their own relationships with dragons.

So, I can't stress enough how important it is to have plants around you. They are of greater benefit to your health than science has yet to understand. Talk to them and spend some time becoming familiar with their vibrations.

MOON GARDENING

If you are living your life in relation to the aspects of the lunar phases then you can also do the same when it comes to planting and harvesting your garden or pot plants. The little verse below will help you remember what to do and when.

The new moon shines for planting herbs and those of leaf and stem.
First quarter shines for planting trees of fruit and bringing seeds.
Full moon she glows for planting bulbs and crops beneath the earth.
The last phase lulls the earth to sleep to harvest and move weeds.

PLANTING CHANT

You can call in the elementals and dragons to aid the growth of your plants, indoors and out, by using this chant:

As above and so below,
May you be blessed to thrive and grow.
By moon and sun by earth and rain,
May Keepers bless this sweet terrain.

HEARTH BLESSING

After you have spent time cleaning up your home, watering, caring for and talking to your plants, filling your cupboards with nourishing food and assembling and decorating your altar in honour of your dragons, it is time to do your home blessing.

This home blessing is a lovely way to conclude your housework tasks and prepare your hearth for dragon magick.

Anoint a candle with the Hearth Blessing Oil. The ingredients for this can be found in Chapter 10. Light it and say:

Dragon guides and dragons of the hearth fire,
Bless our home and all who dwell here,
Fill it with love, harmony, prosperity and cheer.

As we cherish and nurture this sacred space,
Bring good health and kind intentions near,
Protect our home that we hold dear.

Once you are caring for and nourishing yourself and your home, you are then ready to send the same healing and love into the community and out into the world.

You are ready to send out the Hearth Dragon with its heart filled with the joy that you have helped create from your own home and your own heart.

You are ready to help create our kinder New Earth.

CHAPTER 7

The Elements

There are many books that describe the different kinds of dragons that can be encountered and who live on astral and celestial planes. Some reside closer to the earth plane and live within elemental energies.

There are dragons from every continent on the planet that differ from each other in appearance, colours and temperament. They all have different jobs and personalities, much like humans.

This book isn't concerned with describing these aspects to you in detail. There is already a vast choice of literature that will illustrate dragons in all their diverse glory.

I advise that you get to know the dragons who wish to work with you by communicating with them. Research is a helpful tool but it's no substitute for experience.

As the Hearth Dragons practice is concerned mainly with earth magick and elemental energies, I list here some of the ways and natural resources that can be used when working with dragons in your home environment.

Although many dragons, especially the dragons that work as your Hearth Dragons and guides, will reside in and be keepers of more than one element, I'm classifying each individually as a means of simplifying things. Orphus, for example, who is my dragon guide and my Hearth Dragon, resides on a snow-capped mountain that meets the sky. When he comes, he feels like an icy breeze and fills me with a sense of space and freedom. His elements, like his landscape, are earth, water and air, so I can use any of these for communication with him. His predominant colour is white and I've found white and clear crystals are excellent choices for holding during discourse and journeys with him. You can apply this principle to working with your own dragon guide and use corresponding places and objects to amplify your communication.

Mostly you will find that experimenting and seeking solutions together is the best way forward when working with dragons and the elements.

You are the best judge of what to use in your own magick according to your own needs, experiences, location, budget and availability of produce. Whilst all the items mentioned in this book have their own useful energies, the important aspect is always your intent. If you have a strong and focused intent, then you could use a cheese and pickle sandwich and you'd still get good results.

EARTH DRAGONS

Earth dragons are generally gentle but strong-minded. Their colouring is as varied as the earth itself and I've found that they will often change colour depending on mood and season as the leaves of trees will change through the cycle of the year. They can be protectors and healers and also serve to make you self-aware and responsible for your own actions. Their interest is to create balance on earth and dispel the negative energies that would destroy the land and the forests and the creatures that live there.

PLANTS

Herbs that you have grown and harvested yourself are always the best choice to use in any magick, but that's not always possible. I like to use both fresh and dried herbs, bought and grown. I also like to use essential oils and the energy of plants still thriving in the soil. In fact, the latter is by far the most powerful plant energy you will encounter.

There are many choices of herbs that correspond with different intentions. The herbs used in this book are ones chosen because of their magickal properties and the area in which I live. I live in the northern hemisphere in a temperate, somewhat changeable, British climate so I use herbs that are easily obtainable.

This list is a guide only and a tiny sample of what can be used. Use what is available in your location and do research into the magickal properties of your indigenous plants.

- **Lavender** – Calming and healing.
- **Rosemary** – Memory, studying and healing.
- **Silver birch leaves** – Release and decreasing tension.
- **Mugwort** – Communication to other dimensions and psychic awareness.
- **Calendula** – Clarity of mind for bureaucratic tasks, prophetic dreams, healing and protection.
- **Basil** – Prosperity.
- **Mint (all kinds)** – Money, rejuvenation.
- **Lemon balm** – Success, joy, and revitalisation.
- **Bay** – Success and used as a catalyst to other ingredients.
- **Rose petals** – Love, harmony, friendship and relationships.

There are other plants and fruits that are harder to obtain that I also like to use. I buy these in the grocery shop or on the internet.

- **Dragon fruit (freeze-dried)** – Amplifier and enhancer of magickal energy, luck and protection.
- **Lemon (fresh)** – Happiness, hope, rejuvenation and clarity.
- **Pumpkin seeds** – Fertility and creativity.
- **Peppercorns** – Protection and Banishing.

CRYSTALS, ROCKS AND SOIL

Dragons with an earthy vibration will be happy that you have chosen any kind of rock with which to help focus your intent, channel energy or communicate. If you have a rock that you have picked up from a special place, then the resulting joy and memories will help create positive energy for your dragon to ride.

You can also add bowls and jars of soil from special or sacred places to your altar.

If you want to splash out, however, on a beautiful crystal or two, or three, or four ... (I warn you, once you start, you can't stop!) then this list of especially dragon-friendly types and their magickal properties below may help you in your choice.

Obsidian – Elements: earth and fire – 'dragon glass'.

A black, grounding, crystal formed through volcanic lava cooling very quickly and creating its glossy smooth shine. Excellent for use when doing shadow work, and used as a scrying or transfiguration mirror. It calms and heals your energy, brings you back to earth and re-centres your spirit in times of worry. It creates cool clarity in your mind and is an excellent tool of focus when doing waning and dark moon rituals and spell work.

Amethyst – Elements: air and water.

A violet form of quartz, its colour and energies promote calmness and relaxation. It helps open up the crown chakra and promotes spiritual growth, awareness and clarity. It facilitates restful sleep and blocks the path of negative energies. It aids understanding and wisdom. A useful crystal to have close by when studying and meditating.

Hematite – Elements: earth and fire.

This dark, silvery, magnetised, iron oxide crystal is worn to aid the circulatory system and bring confidence and optimism. It promotes balance of energies and grounding. It gives a feeling of safety and protection and is associated with the root chakra for this reason.

Black Tourmaline – Elements: earth and fire.

A black rock that draws out and dispels emotional pain and destructive attitudes. It repairs heart-centred emotions and is therefore connected to the heart chakra. It balances and maintains healthy masculine and feminine energies. It aids shadow work by helping to connect you to your inner self whilst eliminating insecurities. It is protective and deflects negative energies, especially in times of chaos and uncertainty.

Green Jade – Elements: earth.

A soft green crystal that channels energies of growth, health and renewal. It can open the pathways of wealth and prosperity in abundance. A good luck symbol that aids success. A true treasure from the dragon's own cherished collection.

Labradorite – Elements: earth.

This crystal has a flash of colours and sheens. It enhances creative expression, is protective, promotes positive transformation and healing, self-reflection, dispels depression, brings courage, strength and vitality and is useful in manifesting power and success. It is known to promote truth, wisdom and communication and is associated with the throat chakra.

Moonstone – Elements: earth and water.

A moon-coloured stone, often with an adularescence of blues and purples and greens.

Of all the crystals, the moonstone is the one with the most ethereal of qualities. Harnessing the energies of the moon, it can bring both calm and unease, depending on the bearer. It is associated with the divine feminine energy inside all of us and can be used when working to entice the awakening of the kundalini dragon. It is an aid for prophetic dreams and dream communication with dragons. It can soothe stress and balance hormones as well as enhance psychic awareness. The moonstone is associated with the sacral, crown and third eye chakras.

Dragonstone – Elements: earth and fire (blood jasper).

A dark stone with red patches. It is a powerful stone that embodies the vitality and strength of dragons. It promotes creativity, opens the heart chakra and heals the emotional body. It is good for all the chakras and can help awaken the kundalini dragon energy if placed on the crown chakra. It awakens personal power and resolve and brings strength of will. Dragonstone, if carried when searching for a place to live, will aid in connecting you to the right location.

Serpentine – Elements: earth and water.

This crystal is streaked with greens of different hues. It is connected to the energy of the serpent and therefore also of the dragon. Dragons and serpents have always been closely connected, as the wyrms of the Middle Ages were said to be serpent-like dragons with no limbs. This stone is also used as a tool for the awakening of kundalini energy at the base of the spine. Serpentine can be beneficial for clearing all the chakras as the energy rises from the root to the crown.

A powerful yet gentle stone, serpentine is both healing and protective. It can cleanse the auric field and act as a shield against psychic attack.

Selenite – Elements: water and air.

A semi-translucent and white crystallised form of gypsum. This crystal is associated with the moon and has the ability to raise the vibration of anything and anyone in its proximity. It is a good crystal to use to recharge other crystals, the home and yourself. It is highly effective when held in aiding communication with beings from other dimensions and raising your energy to facilitate astral travel and journeys with your dragons. It can be displayed while doing a Hearth Blessing to bring beneficial energy to your home.

Rose Quartz – Elements: earth and water.

A pink crystal that has a gentle, healing energy. When held close to the body, it can bring comfort and reduce physical and mental pain. Rose quartz is the perfect crystal to use in love and friendship spells, home blessings and self-care rituals. Place it in your bath water to promote self-love and healing and in basins of water for cleansing before healing rituals. It promotes gratitude and patience, understanding and empathy. Rose quartz, when placed in the home, encourages harmony and love between those who dwell there.

Clear Quartz – Elements: earth, water and air.

This transparent crystal is the bringer of light to your auric self. It cleanses every chakra and clears negative energy. It uplifts and rejuvenates your spirit and is excellent for use in meditations and communication with dragons to work with you on an intellectual level. It promotes wisdom and clarity in your studies and opens your mind to new inspiration.

As well as being useful in your magickal work, crystals look gorgeous when displayed in a cabinet or in a bowl and can be an uplifting decoration for your home. The way the light dances within them and on their surfaces can only bring joy. They attract dragons because of their vibration and beauty and when coupled with your own energy and intent are an irresistible pull for them.

WATER DRAGONS

Dragons connected with water are of two main types: freshwater and saltwater. Both have different properties. Saltwater dragons tend to be enormous as they have the expanse of the oceans in which to dwell and grow; and the freshwater types that languish in lakes, lochs and rivers are often serpent-like in appearance. Both have a cool, aloofness and tend to keep themselves to themselves, if possible. They are concerned mainly with the healing and cleansing of the waters of our planet, the irrigation of the land and the hydration of its creatures.

VISITS TO THE SEA AND LAKES

Water dragons are connected to the energies of the moon and the colour silver. They love the play of silver sunlight that dances on waves when the sun is low over the water, and the moonlight of a full moon on a clear night. So, if you are ever near an expanse of water at these times, you can ask the water dragons to show themselves. You may just see the flick of a tail and the splash of water or they may give you a clear mental image of themselves when you close your eyes. Look also at the shadows that pass over the water that seem to come from nowhere and the reflections within.

If you feel a strong connection to the water dragon when you are near lakes and sea shores, then you can collect shells, small pebbles, seaweed (dry this in the sun first to eliminate smell and rotting) and small phials of the water. These can be displayed and used in your spells and rituals when you are back at home and the energies they hold will help recall the power of the dragons.

You can also use sea salt as a protective element for your Circle. I sprinkle tiny amounts on window sills, garden paths and external doorsteps to protect my home while I'm away.

If you do this, you can use this chant while you sprinkle:

Sea Salt Protection Chant

With salt of the sea, I call upon the power of the ocean and its dragons to protect my home from all harm.

My home was broken into once but the intruder stole nothing and left in a hurry, leaving running footprints in the snow and then jumped the fence to land through the ice of next-door's pond. Justice of the watery kind indeed. I often wonder what had startled this person so much to leave in this manner, but I have an inkling ...

We don't all have access to oceans and lakes, but all water, everywhere, has its own magick. Water is a fabulous conductor of energy. We know this because of the dangers of water and electricity. But it can also conduct energy from your dragons.

I was surprised to find that the structure and contents of this book were downloaded into my head, bit by bit, every time I had a shower. As soon as I was immersed in the water sprays, the information came. So, I can't really take much credit at all for the writing of it.

Take note next time you are bathing, showering or walking in the rain and you will most likely find that inspiration and knowledge seem to arrive in your brain. If you work with dragons, they will make the most of any situation to provide you with instructions and motivation in creating positive changes.

Simple basins of water can be used for purifying, healing, divination and shadow work. There are endless possibilities and uses for water and your dragons, if you ask, will give you ideas on how they want to work through it.

A glass of drinking water, if imbued with dragon healing energy, can become medicine. A cup of tea can become an aid to spell work and washing your hair can become a means of dragon communication. Never underestimate the power of everyday life and just how much magick there is in ordinary things.

FIRE DRAGONS

Of all the dragons, the fire dragon is the one that's had a very bad press throughout generations of human storytelling.

I have, so far, only met one, face to face, in my meditations. He was very large, red, and had tiny yellow eyes with a pinprick of a pupil. He looked, in fact, much as I would expect a fire dragon to look. He said nothing at all but searched my mind as he held my gaze with his intense stare. He read me, puffed smoke from his nostrils and then vanished. I don't think he was too impressed but I've felt him around during my banishing and release spells with candle flame and charcoal and maybe, one day, he will talk to me … or maybe he doesn't need to. Maybe he is just the strong, silent type … and that's ok.

Fire dragon energy can be protective and purifying, as in the use of smoke for smudging and cleansing and flames for burning and banishing. This warrior energy is perfect for facing challenges, finding courage and fuelling passions and intense creativity. When you need an extra kick up the backside to get on with something or to get rid of something and face changes, then fire dragons will be your allies. If you are facing a bully or a situation that is fearsome, then you can call on these magnificent creatures to stand by you. They will not harm another soul on your behalf. That is not their job. But they may well protect and defend you by making you aware of your own power.

SMOKE AND FLAME MANIFESTATION

Fire dragons can make an appearance within flames and smoke.

Try looking into the flame of a candle, a hearth fire or fire pit and ask if a fire dragon will show itself to you. Let your mind drift a little and let your gaze soften and look through the flames and smoke. Listen to the guidance in your heart and your sight will be drawn to a particular place. Be patient and respectful and the dragon will show itself within the light and flicker of the fire or in the swirling smoke formations.

Stay safe. Be careful and responsible with fire. Fire, like its dragon, is untamed and should be handled with respect and caution.

AIR DRAGONS

Air dragons, like the sky, are rapidly changeable. They can be enormous and span the stars, or small, alert and agile. All dragons can change colour, shape and size at will, but the air dragons can disperse and drift as summer clouds or spread wings that lift their solid forms that flash like ice and steel.

Air dragons can be elusive and playful and love freedom above all else. They are wise and insightful, their perspective of life being unencumbered with small trivialities. Air dragons are drawn to creativity and learning. If you want help with research and studies and artistic endeavours, then the air dragons are the ones to call upon.

They can be seen in the clouds, in plumes of smoke (along with their fellows, the fire dragons) and as vast shadows crossing the moon and stars at night. They can make homes in high places and are happy in mountains and above the canopy of forests. They love expanses of space where they can fly freely and swiftly. Their breath can be as cold as a December wind and if one comes close to you, you will feel the temperature suddenly drop around you.

The air dragon likes to communicate about things of importance. Don't bother it with your mundane concerns. As big as these concerns may be to you, the air dragon will only tolerate discourse of this nature if it is required to resolve a greater matter. It will aid you in your magickal journey and help you in personal matters, but only as a means to guide you to your true path, towards bringing the kinder New Earth.

The air dragon wishes to breathe pure, clean air and this means bringing changes towards a greener environment and an enlightened human race. The winds of transformation are its concern.

And this brings us to weather magick.

WEATHER MAGICK

Weather magick has been a matter of some controversy within the communities of humans who work with and manipulate energy. It has been labelled as 'dark magick' and we are often advised not to dabble with it. Whatever your views of weather magick, there is no doubt that it is a truly fascinating area of study but not one to be taken lightly. If you view the weather as simply another powerful form of energy, then it is sensible to assume that it can be transformed through interference from other energies. With practice, it is possible to shift the weather in an intended direction. If an air dragon or other sky spirit is working with you, then you know that the consequences of your intentions are likely to be huge.

Messing about with the weather should therefore probably only be considered as a last resort to solve a problem of magnitude, or maybe never considered at all.

I was once part of an online group of witches that banded together to create a spell that would shift rain clouds to Australia during the time of the wide-spreading fires. There were a lot of us involved who were very concerned about the destruction of animals and people and their homes. We created spells for rain in that area and the rain did come. We were happy to feel we had helped but the truth is that we really didn't know if we'd caused more disruption elsewhere. There were tsunamis, storms and freak weather conditions happening in other areas. You can't alter one aspect of nature without it affecting the whole globe.

But then that can be argued with pretty much every decision we ever make about anything. There are always consequences to our thoughts and actions and the only thing we really have any control over are our intentions. As long as our intentions are good ones then we can't be held responsible for everything that may or may not happen in the ripple effect across the universe.

And maybe the rain clouds bursting over Australia wasn't down to us at all. It could well have been nature's own reaction to the spread of smoke in the atmosphere, or the rain may have already been heading there anyway. We will never know, but my point here is that we need to be aware that whatever we do, and especially when working with magick, energy and a will of change, there is a great possibility that whatever we are trying to achieve just might happen. And it will, without a shadow of a doubt, happen in ways that we never expected.

The truth is that we never really know what the consequences are going to be from transforming energy from one thing to another. Metaphorically speaking, as well as literally, as we light that candle and chant our intentions while calling on dragons and spirits, we have to accept that the shower of rain we wish for to stop the drought, might just create a more destructive flood.

Whatever you choose to do, be aware of unforeseen consequences. Search for wisdom before you act and always ask for guidance from your dragon and spirit guides.

That being said, here are a couple of spells to bring rain if you need them. Orphus, my spirit team, and I have used them to good effect (as far as we know) in times of great need. What you decide to do is up to you and your conscience.

Magick itself is never black or white.

SKY DRAGON SPELL TO BRING RAIN

You will need:
- Wand.
- Dry fern leaves.
- Charcoal disc and fireproof bowl/mini cauldron.
- Matches.

➢ **Open and seal your Circle out of doors.**

This works so much better outside where you can feel and address the sky dragons and spirits directly. So, if possible, do this outside in a private space.

- Use your wand to draw the Circle of light around you while you say the usual opening prayer.
- Set alight the charcoal and add the dried fern leaves.

Say:

> From fern and fire let smoke rise high
> Carry my intention into the sky.

- Then point your wand towards the sky and expand your personal energy so that you are no longer just pointing at the sky but you are part of it – part of its vastness. Listen to the sounds of any wind or birds. Move the wand slowly in a clockwise circle above you.
- Say, or preferably sing:

> Dragons of wind and sky and sea,
> Carry the rain to ...... (place name), I plea.
> Let rain travel quickly, falling free,
> To quench the land. So mote it be.

Feel the pull of your wand through the air and the movement of energy it creates. Connect with this movement. Watch for visible shifts and strands of energy. Maybe the light changes around you or maybe you can feel changes to the air on your skin. Open your senses, all of them, to any subtle differences, as you pull your wand through the sky. Imagine the rain falling wherever it is that you intend it to be. See it and smell and feel it as it hits the earth and drenches the dry soil. Make it real inside your mind, while still being aware of the changes around you where you stand.

➢ **Close your Circle as usual.**

➢ **Eat and drink your refreshments to help ground yourself.**

➢ **Record the spell and future outcomes in your magickal journal.**

I have noticed the wind suddenly rising around me and the air becoming dense, if the intent is for rain at home. The clouds come slowly.

My guides and I have not always been over-successful. Once during a lengthy drought, we managed to bring one solitary rain cloud over the roof of my home, which looked quite amusing, but on other occasions, there has been a dramatic shift from blue skies and scorching sun to the rising wind that brings grey clouds and cool rain.

The changing climate has brought unfamiliar weather patterns across the globe. Maybe there will be more of us resorting to weather magick as the climate changes become more severe.

On occasions, when I have worked with air dragons, there have been enormous energy faces that appear in the sky. Not cloud formations, but clear, precise transfiguration-like changes, where features and details have clarity of form. I have seen sky spirits in full headdresses as well as dragons. I've tried to take photos but, sadly, they never come out well. But that's ok. The images, I feel are there to encourage me in my work, and that's exactly what they do.

I have heard of Tibetan monks using a horn made from a human thigh bone to play a sound that removes rainclouds from the sky and ensures a sunny day for celebration feasts outdoors.

I don't have a human thigh bone horn but maybe a regular instrument or song could do the same to entice air dragons to temporarily shift rainclouds away. I've never tried. If you want to try this, then have a chat with your dragon guide first. It would make an interesting experiment.

CHAPTER 8

Dragon Quest Eggs

O rphus planted and hatched this idea in my head and together we have been sending energy eggs of positive intent wherever needed.

The process is a creative but simple one and you need to talk to your dragon guide first to find out if they are willing to work with you to deliver these eggs.

The use of colour magick is an important aspect of these quests, and both physical and visualised colour is used.

You can send anything you like, as long it has a positive intent and no harm comes to anyone and you aren't bending anyone's will. It's also a good idea to get permission from the intended receiver(s) first, but there are occasions when this isn't possible. You'll need to decide for yourself what's best in these situations.

The dragon eggs and the quests are manifested in your mind.

- Decide first on what you need the egg for.
- Visualise the details of its appearance and where it is going and why. Who is it for? Why is it needed? How quickly does this egg need to hatch? Is it meant as a long-term, slow release or a quick burst of energy? Communicate all of these thoughts with your dragon.
- Draw or paint the egg in your magickal journal and when you are clear in your mind of the egg's purpose, write everything down in your journal. Then summarise the intention into one word and form a sigil.
- Draw the sigil onto the egg in your journal, then draw it onto the egg in your mind.
- You will by now have a clear mental picture of your egg and its purpose.
- Now close your eyes and hold your egg in your hands. Feel the weight of it and the vibration of positive energy growing inside it. See it shining brightly with all the love you have put into it.

- Pass it to your dragon who will carry it to its destination and it will hatch and the energy within will pour out to help those that dwell, work in or visit that space.

Your dragon will have its own means of carrying the egg to its destination. You may want to watch the egg being delivered and hatching or you may be content to let the dragon complete the quest without you while you eat cake and drink tea. Either way is fine.

Orphus takes the egg from me by absorbing it into his chest and heart area. There it glows within him and he takes off like a winged lantern to deliver his precious cargo. I trust him to get on with it without my interference from this point.

I have included here a few examples and listed instructions on how the dragon egg quest can be used to further the Hearth Dragon Philosophy and send positive energy to individuals and into the community.

DRAGON EGG – TO HEAL THE EARTH.

This is a lovely quest that can be done by numerous people from their own homes during a particular moon phase. It's a good community or coven activity and the healing energy will be all the more powerful when a group of like-minded people become involved.

Moon Phase: Full or new moon.

You will need:
- Your prepared altar space.
- An offering of refreshment for your dragon's return.
- Your magickal journal.
- Art tools of your choice – pens, paint, coloured paper, etc.
- Sigil – Create your own, or use the Healing Sigil illustrated in Chapter 2.

- Draw an outline of an egg on a page in your magickal journal.
- Decorate it and colour it with healing colours. Soft greens and blues are good for this and they also represent the Earth.
- Give it time to dry before you open your Circle for the work.
- Open your Circle in the usual way.
- On another page in your journal, write the intent of the egg and where it is going. In this case:

To Heal the Earth ...

To spread positive love and enlightenment to all people. To rid the Earth of cruelty and unnecessary suffering. To allow nature to thrive and the land, water and sky to be free of harmful substances. To allow peace within communities and between nations and the freedom to live simply.

This egg will spread its light and love throughout the entire globe.

- If you are creating your own sigil, you can then simplify the intent to 'Heal Earth' and then once more to H.E. Use the letters to form the basis of your sigil.
- Focus on your intent and visualise how your kinder New Earth will be. Communicate your thoughts with your dragon and be open to their ideas and wishes.
- Draw the sigil on the egg. Make it large and clear and keep the intent in mind as you draw it.

- Close your eyes and visualise this egg in your hands. Feel its weight, its size and its glowing colours. See the sigil burning brightly on its shell. The egg vibrates with love and healing. It is warm and alive. Imagine where it will be going.
- When you are ready, pass the egg to your dragon. Your dragon will take the egg and deliver it to where it needs to go.
- Thank your dragon, watch it leave and know in your heart that the egg will be placed in the best possible situation for the energy to hatch out and spread its positive intent to those who need it.
- Open your eyes and feel gratitude for what has been achieved.
- Close your Circle.
- Refresh yourself with food and drink. Have a tasty treat ready for your dragon for their return.

DRAGON EGG – TO SEND PROTECTION

This quest can help send powerful protective energy to those who do not live with you or who are travelling away from you.

Moon Phase: When needed but full moon is best.

You will need:
- Your prepared altar space.
- An offering of refreshment for your dragon's return.
- Your magickal journal.
- Art tools of your choice – pens, paint, coloured paper, etc.

- Sigil – Create your own, or use the Protection Sigil illustrated in Chapter 2.
- Draw an outline of an egg on a page in your magickal journal.
- Decorate it and colour it with protective colours. Dark, earthy colours and black work well with steely greys and silver.
- Give it time to dry before you cast your Circle for the work.
- Open your Circle in the usual way.
- On another page in your journal, write the intent of the egg and where it is going. In this case:

To Send Protection ...

To spread positive, protective energy to those in need. Repel all forces of harm and surround with protective light.

This egg will spread its light and protective love to surround ...... (add name and address here) and keep them safe from any harm.

- If you are creating your own sigil, you can then simplify this to 'Protection and Safety' and then once more to P.S. Use the letters to form the basis of your sigil.
- Focus on your intent and visualise the receiver(s) surrounded with protective energy and light. Communicate your thoughts with your dragon and be open to their ideas and wishes.
- Draw the sigil on the egg. Make it large and clear and keep the intent in mind as you draw it.

- Close your eyes and visualise this egg in your hands. Feel its weight, its size and its glowing colours. See the sigil burning brightly on its shell. The egg vibrates with protective energy. It is warm and alive. Imagine where it will be going.
- When you are ready, pass the egg to your dragon. Your dragon will take the egg and deliver it to where it needs to go.
- Thank your dragon, watch it leave and know in your heart that the egg will be placed in the best possible situation for the energy to hatch out and surround those who need it with protection.
- Open your eyes and feel gratitude for what has been achieved.
- Close your Circle.
- Refresh yourself with food and drink. Have a tasty treat ready for your dragon for their return.

DRAGON EGG – TO SEND DISTANT HEALING.

This egg quest is perfect to help those who need healing that are far away or maybe to send to a household where there is more than one person or animal that requires healing. This can be used for physical, emotional and mental healing, but is not a substitute for Earthly medicine. It's a gentle way to add to existing medical support.

Moon Phase: Any. Send whenever needed.

You will need:

- Your prepared altar space.
- An offering of refreshment for your dragon's return.
- Your magickal journal.
- Art tools of your choice – pens, paint, coloured paper, etc.
- Sigil – Create your own, or use the Healing Sigil illustrated in Chapter 2.

- Draw an outline of an egg on a page in your magickal journal.
- Decorate it and colour it with healing colours. Soft greens, blues and violets with silver.
- Give it time to dry before you open your Circle for the work.
- Open your Circle in the usual way.
- On another page in your journal, write the intent of the egg and where it is going. In this case:

To Send Distant Healing …

To spread positive healing of mind and body to all beings that require it. To spread violet, blue and green light to dispel harmful energies and replace them with healing and love and the silver light of rejuvenation, good health and the wisdom and means to maintain it.

This egg will spread its healing light and love to …… (add name and address).

- If you are creating your own sigil, you can then simplify this to 'Heal' and then once more to H.L. Use the letters to form the basis of your sigil.
- Focus on your intent and visualise the healing. Communicate your thoughts with your dragon and be open to their ideas and wishes.
- Draw the sigil on the egg. Make it large and clear and keep the intent in mind as you draw it.
- Close your eyes and visualise this egg in your hands. Feel its weight, its size and its glowing colours. See the sigil burning brightly on its shell. The egg vibrates with love and healing. It is warm and alive. Imagine where it will be going.
- When you are ready, pass the egg to your dragon. Your dragon will take the egg and deliver it to where it needs to go.
- Thank your dragon, watch it leave and know in your heart that the egg will be placed in the best possible situation for the energy to hatch out and spread its positive healing to those who need it.
- Open your eyes and feel gratitude for what has been achieved.
- Close your Circle.
- Refresh yourself with food and drink. Have a tasty treat ready for your dragon for their return.

DRAGON EGG – TO SEND LOVE & HARMONY.

This quest can be used to send love and harmony to a workplace, or any place that needs a little help in banishing discord and toxicity.

Moon Phase: Waning or dark moon.

You will need:

- Your prepared altar space.
- An offering of refreshment for your dragon's return.
- Your magickal journal.
- Art tools of your choice – pens, paint, coloured paper, etc.
- Sigil – Create your own, or use the Love & Harmony Sigil illustrated in Chapter 2.

- Draw an outline of an egg on a page in your magickal journal.
- Decorate it and colour it with golds and purples.
- Give it time to dry before you open your Circle for the work.
- Open your Circle in the usual way.
- On another page in your journal, write the intent of the egg and where it is going. In this case:

To Send Love & Harmony …

First, purify and cleanse the area and dispel all negative and harmful energies. Fill the area with violet light to heal the space. Then spread positive golden energy full of love and harmony into every corner. This energy will linger and infuse all who work there with feelings of harmony and compassion for each other.

This egg will spread its light and love throughout ...... (add the name and address).

- If you are creating your own sigil, you can then simplify this to 'Love Harmony' and then once more to L.H. Use the letters to form the basis of your sigil.
- Focus on your intent and visualise how your chosen space will benefit from this energy. How will harmony and love make a difference, and to whom? Communicate your thoughts with your dragon and be open to their ideas and wishes.
- Draw the sigil on the egg. Make it large and clear and keep the intent in mind as you draw it.
- Close your eyes and visualise this egg in your hands. Feel its weight, its size and its glowing colours. See the sigil burning brightly on its shell. The egg vibrates with love and harmony. It is warm and alive. Imagine where it will be going.
- When you are ready, pass the egg to your dragon. Your dragon will take the egg and deliver it to where it needs to go.
- Thank your dragon, watch it leave and know in your heart that the egg will be placed in the best possible situation for the energy to hatch out and spread its positive intent to those who need it.
- Open your eyes and feel gratitude for what has been achieved.
- Close your Circle.
- Refresh yourself with food and drink. Have a tasty treat ready for your dragon for their return.

CHAPTER 9

Manifestation Spells for Earthly Desires

Our earthly desires could be seen as selfish needs, but in order to be able to help others, we must first help ourselves. This doesn't mean that we should fill our boots with greed and want, but it does mean that if we are comfortable, happy and free of suffering, we will be much better channels for energy for other causes. It is for this reason that dragons will intervene and help you out. If they can see that your reasons for needing help are just a small piece of a larger picture, then they will be more likely to oblige. As we have already discussed, in order to help the Hearth Dragons fly with positive intent for the community and the New Earth, we must first serve our own self-care and that of our hearth.

For this reason, I have included spells for some of the more necessary aspects of human life.

For all spells, cleanse yourself and your space and purify all tools, herbs, crystals and oils before you use them by using your small bell and the purification chant in Chapter 2.

EARTH DRAGON, CHOCOLATE & ROSES LOVE SPELL BAG

Dragons, chocolate and roses ... what finer ingredients for love could anyone want?

Chocolate creates endorphins in our bodies that make us feel good. These can be utilised in personal energy and magick and are especially potent for love spells.

Intention: To bring a new lover/companion who is loyal and true (for yourself or for another).

Moon Phase: Full or new moon.

You will need:
- Your prepared altar space.
- A pink or white candle anointed with Dragon Rose Oil.
- Chocolates in wrappers (so it is covered when inside the bag if giving to a third party).
- A small bag with a drawstring.
- An offering for your dragon (chocolate maybe?).
- Your magickal journal and pen.
- Crystals: Rose quartz (a small piece for the bag).

- Herbs: Dried rose petals, dried lavender.
- Oils & Teas: Dragon Rose Oil.
- Sigils: Create your own, or use the Love & Harmony Sigil illustrated in Chapter 2.

➤ **Open your Circle as usual.**

➤ **The Spell**

Light your anointed candle.
- Place the chocolate, sigil, rose quartz, rose petals, lavender and small bag in front of it.
- Point your wand at the items and say:

> I charge these items with the energy of love,
> May they find love and bring love.

- Then put them into the bag, one by one, and say:

> Rose quartz to bring comfort.
> Rose petals to bring passion.
> Lavender to bring gentleness.
> Chocolate to sweeten their path.
> The sigil to bind them in synergy.
> Dragon guide and Earth dragons, I ask for your aid and wisdom in bringing the right person to me (or the name of the person you are doing the spell for).

- Eat one of the chocolates and hold the filled bag in your hand.

- Visualise the type of person you are going to attract.
- Vocalise the attributes you want in a partner (for yourself or a third party).
- If the spell is for yourself, say this chant:

To the one who is loyal and true.

Your steps will tread my pathway soon,
By the light of fullest moon.
Your kindness and your beauty shine,
Your conversation flows like wine.

With honesty, your words to tell,
With love, respect, you treat me well.
You brighten both my night and day,
And yours I brighten my own way.

You ride this way, our paths will cross,
With all to gain and ne'er a loss.
The stars will guide you on your way,
By fullest moon with no delay.

Love will come.

(If the spell is for another person, then they must say the chant after you have given them the bag, so have a copy of it ready to give to them.)

➢ **Close your Circle in the usual way.**

➢ **Eat and drink your refreshments to help ground yourself.**

➢ **Record the spell and future outcomes in your magickal journal.**

If the spell bag is for another person, then give them the bag. They can eat the chocolate while envisaging their new partner and keep the rest of the items in the bag in a safe place. They will act as a talisman.

If the spell bag is for you, do the same.

Trust that the dragons will, if it is the right time and for the right reasons, help to find a suitable person.

AIR DRAGON INSPIRATION SONG

Intention: To bring inspiration.

Moon Phase: new moon.

You will need:
- Your prepared altar space.
- A white candle anointed with Hearth Dragon Oil.
- An offering for your dragon.
- Your magickal journal and pen.

➢ **Open your Circle as usual.**

➢ **The Spell**
- Light your anointed candle and say:
   Dragon Guide and Dragons of the air,
   I ask for your help, your wisdom and creativity,
   In finding the inspiration that I need for ... (add
      in here whatever it is you need inspiration for).
- Watch the candle flame and smoke for a few seconds and then say or sing:

Inspiration Song

As I set my mind adrift,
I sail to shores as yet unseen.
And so, I find new lands of wonder,
Grey blue seas and forests green.

Within the shadow of the trees,
A spark of white glows like a star.
A new idea that spreads its light,
It comes towards me from afar.

And as it nears me, I can tell,
My inspiration follows well.

And as it nears me, I can tell,
My inspiration follows well.

My inspiration follows.

- Now sit quietly and let your dragon help you release all the ideas that are already with you and let in all the new ideas that can be given.
- Write anything down that comes to mind in your magickal journal.

➤ **Close your Circle as usual.**

➤ **Eat and drink your refreshments to help ground yourself.**

➤ **Record the spell and future outcomes in your magickal journal.**

GOLDEN DRAGON ABUNDANCE ORIGAMI

Please practice making the dragon origami before you do the spell. There are lots of excellent videos on YouTube to try, so please find one you are happy using and try it out a few times. The finished paper dragons are very beautiful and you could put together a whole collection of magickally charged dragons and hang them in your home. I like to decorate the paper with watercolours in relevant colours before I use them for spells, but thin wrapping paper can also be used, or you could purchase some pretty origami paper.

Intention: To bring an abundance of wealth.

Moon Phase: Full or waxing moon.

You will need:
- On your phone: A YouTube instruction video for an origami dragon (if you can memorise how to make it beforehand then that would be even better).
- Thin paper exactly square: 20 x 20cm or larger.
- A gold pen.
- Your prepared altar space.
- An offering for your dragon.
- Your magickal journal and pen.
- Crystals: Green Jade.
- Herbs: None used but a bunch of basil on your altar will smell gorgeous and bring helpful vibrations.
- Oils & Teas: Golden Dragon Success and Abundance Oil.

- Sigils: Create your own, or use the Prosperity Sigil illustrated in Chapter 2.

➢ **Open your Circle as usual.**

➢ **The Spell**

- Light your anointed candle.
- Place the green jade on top of your open paper on your altar.
- Call in your dragon guide and the energy of the golden dragon to help you.
- Say:

I call on the dragon of wealth and abundance,
Lend me your golden wings of financial health.
My bank account fills with funds in abundance,
I deserve to have freedom and financial wealth.

No more will I suffer, for need of some money,
No more will I worry, the bills I can pay.
My life now is comfort and sweeter than honey,
And harm comes to no one, as funds come my way.

- Remove the jade and place it back on your altar.
- Draw your sigil on the paper with your golden pen.
- When dry, fold the paper (with the help of the YouTube video) into the dragon.
- As you fold the paper, visualise your life with the money you need. Imagine your bank account, your bank statement, with the funds all there.

- What is it you need it for? Imagine this has already happened. How does it feel?
- As you create your dragon, fold all the positive thoughts into its neck, wings and tail.
- When you have finished, place it on your altar and sit quietly for a few moments to admire it.
- Thank the golden dragon for helping and say farewell.

➢ **Close your Circle as usual.**

➢ **Eat & drink your refreshments to help ground yourself.**

➢ **Record the spell and future outcomes in your magickal journal.**

When done, you can sit your paper dragon on a shelf or hang him up in your house. If you prefer, you can keep him safe in a special box.

AIR DRAGON SUCCESS SPELL JAR

Intention: Success (in whatever you need at the time).

Moon Phase: Full or waxing moon.

You will need:
- Your prepared altar space.
- Orange or white candle anointed with Golden Dragon Success & Abundance Oil.
- An offering for your dragon.
- Your magickal journal and pen.
- A small, clean glass jar.

- **Crystals:** A small piece of jade.
- **Dried Herbs:** (must be dried or they will go mouldy over time) Bay leaf, lemon balm and an herb that resonates with your particular type of success:
- **Mint, Basil** for Money and Career.
- **Calendula** for Legal Matters.
- **Pumpkin Seeds** for Fertility & Creative Projects.
- **Rosemary, Mint** for Academic Success.
- **Oils & Teas:** Golden Dragon Success & Abundance Oil.
- Sigils: Create your own, or use the Abundance & Prosperity Sigil illustrated in Chapter 2.

➢ **Open your Circle as usual.**

➢ **The Spell**
  - Light your anointed candle and invite in the golden dragon of success and abundance with this verse:

    Golden Dragon please hear my voice,
    And aid success in my path of choice.
    Give golden light and power to me,
    To bring about my destiny.

    With this success my way is clear,
    To help this Earth that I hold dear.

  - Now fill the jar with the herbs and vocalise your own intent as you do so.
  - Place the piece of jade and the sigil inside the jar and put the lid on.

- Hold the jar in your hands and visualise your life as if the success you wish for has already happened. How does it feel? How has your life changed? What happens now in your journey?
- Thank the golden dragon and say farewell. Let feelings of gratitude rise within you and into the jar.

➤ **Close your Circle in the usual way.**

➤ **Eat and drink your refreshments to help ground yourself.**

➤ **Record the spell and future outcomes in your magickal journal.**

You can keep the jar for as long as you feel necessary. You might like to decorate and display it to remind you of your rising success or you may prefer to store it away safely. If you need to use the jade stone again, then it's ok to remove it after a little while and use it for another purpose. The intent is still within the jar.

Dragons will help you with your path of success as long as you are putting in the work yourself. Don't sit back and wait. Do whatever needs to be done to bring your goal in to fruition.

WATER DRAGON HEALING OF A LOVED ONE

This is healing for a third party who is sympathetic to your dragon witchcraft and who will not be phased by being present during a ritual.

Intention: To bring healing energies for those in need.

Moon Phase: Waning moon or whenever needed.

You will need:
- A basin of spring or filtered water (large enough to put your hands in).
- Two glasses of drinking water.
- Your prepared altar space.
- A comfortable resting place for the recipient of the healing.
- An offering for your dragon.
- Your magickal journal and pen.
- Crystals: Rose quartz.
- Herbs: Rosemary (fresh if possible).

➢ **Open your Circle in the usual way.**

➢ **The Healing**
- Ensure your third party (person receiving the healing) is comfortably seated and wearing comfortable clothing.
- Ask them to breathe slowly and deeply and relax.
- Place the water vessels beside your altar.
- Light your candles and incense, if you haven't done so already.
- Add rosemary and rose quartz to the basin of water and bless it by saying:

  I add these elements of Earth to purify and positively charge this water with healing energy.

- When you are both ready, invite the dragons by saying:

Dragons of the elements, our guides and friends
draw near.
Your breath transforms to medicine,
This water pure and clear.
I seek your diagnosis and your unique energy,
To heal both mind and body,
And restore the vital chi.

- Inform the recipient that you will be entering a light trance-like state in order to channel dragon energy to facilitate healing.
- Ask them to breathe slowly and deeply and relax.

(Refer here to the section on Trance Work in Chapter 1 to prepare yourself as a receiving vessel for the energies.)

You can either hold your hands over the water vessels to channel directly through yourself into the water or use your wand by pointing at each in turn.

The water may or may not appear different. It may have changed visually. It may have changed temperature or consistency. It may look exactly the same. Trust that the dragons have done what is necessary and have breathed whatever elemental energy is required to heal the ailment.

Wash your hands in the water basin and dry them with the clean towel.

Place your hands on or over the area requiring healing and invite the dragons to restore the area to health.

If the ailments are emotional or mental, then place one hand over the crown area and the other over the solar plexus (ensure your recipient is ok with this. Explain that they may feel energies within their bodies and that this is normal and necessary).

If at any time the recipient is unhappy with any of the process, then it must be immediately stopped. The dragons will step back when asked to do so and so must you.

The recipient is in control at all times.

Use your judgement to determine how long the healing needs to be. When you feel that the dragons have finished, or when they have instructed you to finish, thank them and check on your recipient.

You may both drink your glasses of charged water at this point and feel the benefit of its healing energy.

Rest for a while until you are both feeling grounded and able to function normally.

- ➢ **Close your Circle as usual.**

- ➢ **Eat and drink your refreshments (both you and the recipient).**

- ➢ **Record the healing and future outcomes in your magickal journal.**

CHAPTER 10

Oils and Teas

These oils and teas had been described to me through meditations with Orphus when we first began to communicate and are the ones that we use in our work together. Remember intention is everything, so keep your intended use for them in mind as you create them and use them. Your intention is what fully activates the ingredients and, trust me, they can be very powerful indeed. I am always reminded of the way my dog could activate healing energy from plants in the garden. We too can do this.

Oil blends and infusions are always welcome additions to any kind of magick.

They are a tactile, practical use of plant, water and oil energies. They add great focus to your intention in a physical way.

Teas can be ingested before or during a meditation or spell or ritual, so that the magickal intention spreads through your body. Or they can be used in healing and ritual baths, in compresses and to anoint tools and yourself.

Oils can be used to anoint candles with a specific intent and in diffusers and oil burners for ritual and spell work, so that the air itself is filled with the intent of your magick.

Mixing your own blends will add a special element of love and care from your own energies which will enhance your magick. When you call in the energy of your dragons, this will boost the effects even further.

ENERGY CHARGING THE TEA

When making your blend of tea, be fully present in your mind as you add each ingredient.

Pull energy into your body from the earth and the air, call in your dragon guide and ask for its help.

Name each ingredient as it is added and what its intended purpose is.

When you have finished making your tea blend and it is stored in a dark, air-tight jar, or if you are making just one cup and it sits steeping in hot water, put your hands around the vessel containing it.

Pull energy into your body from the earth and the air, call in your dragon guide and ask for its help.

Vocalise the intent of the tea and as you do so channel the energy you have pulled in from the earth, air and dragon and let it flow through your arms and hands into the tea.

Imagine this energy as white light or a bright colour, one that reflects your intention, and watch it surround and enter your tea. It shines and vibrates with this positive energy and is now ready to drink and it fills you with the power to manifest your goals.

If you have filled a tea caddy with the herbs, then you can add a label and adorn the cannister with dragon images or charms. When you make a brew from your tea blend, you can use the energy exercise again to re-charge the cup of tea.

ENERGY CHARGING THE OIL

As with the tea, call in the help of your dragon and be present in naming each oil as you add it to your blend and vocalise each oil's intended magickal use.

Channel the dragon energy and that of the earth and air into the bottle as described for making the tea, then you can label and decorate your bottle with a dragon charm.

Labelling the vessels with these symbols will further charge the ingredients with the energy required.

This channelling exercise can also be used to charge up any object you desire, tools, clothing, crystals, food, water, jewellery ... anything you might need to infuse with an extra boost of power.

You can further charge the tea and oils by creating and using them during their specific moon phases.

TEAS

DRAGON WING TEA.

For flying with dragons.

Moon Phase: Waxing and full moon.

Ingredients: Dried herbs – equal amounts of each:

Mint – For clarity of mind and safe travel.
Black Tea – Alertness and raised energy levels.
Dragon Fruit (freeze-dried is fine, but crumble it up) – Enhanced connection with your dragon.
Mugwort – For insight and spiritual flight, wards off negative energies.

When brewed, add a quarter slice of fresh lemon to each cup. This will invigorate you and your taste buds and bring more enjoyment to the experience.

This tea isn't called Dragon Wing Tea for nothing. It really can help you fly. It is very refreshing and can make you feel a little light-headed and very relaxed, so make sure you have set up everything you need before you drink it. Sip it slowly. You only need a small cup with one level teaspoon of the blend in your tea diffuser. Let it steep for 3 minutes in boiled water.

DRAGON DREAM TEA.

To bring dragon communication through your dreams.
Moon Phase: Waning moon. Especially on a dark moon.

Ingredients: Dried herbs – equal amounts of each:

Mint – For clarity of mind and safe travel.

Chamomile – Re-energising sleep.

Lavender – Wards off negative energy and brings positive, peaceful, connections with the astral realm.

Mugwort – Prophetic dreams and spiritual insight.

OILS

HEARTH DRAGON MEDITATION OIL.

Moon Phase: Full or waxing moon.

Gaining wisdom and action to bring the New Earth.

This is a lovely aromatic oil to be used in an oil burner with a drop of water. The scent invigorates the mind and helps you tune in with your dragon guide during the meditation.

The meditation itself is very simple. Sit quietly, with no distractions and ask your dragon guide to give you more information on how to serve the Hearth Dragon philosophy. Your dragon may have something special in mind for you both in your quest to bring a kinder New Earth.

This oil can also be used to help you in your other spiritual research, studies and creativity. Just add it to your oil burner while you read or listen to audio-books, watch documentaries or create new rituals and spells.

Ingredients: Essential Oils – equal amounts of each:

Rosemary – Remembering, concentration.

Bay – Study success, positive thinking.

Scott's Pine – Mental clarity, open-mindedness, refreshes and clears negative thoughts.

Frankincense – Spiritual awakening, connection, insight and understanding.

Add the base oil – 10x the total quantity of the other oils.

Olive oil – Love and harmony.

If possible, leave the oil in some sunlight for 20 minutes and ask the sun to charge it with fire energy for positive action and thought.

You can also leave it outside for the night to charge under the full moonlight. Call on the moon to enhance wisdom and awakening.

HEARTH BLESSING OIL.

Moon Phase: Waning or dark moon.

Used to anoint the candle during your home blessing prayer.

Ingredients: Essential Oils – equal amounts of each:

Rosemary – Healing.

Lavender – Calmness and harmony.

Rose – Deep love, care and nurturing.

Basil – Prosperity.

Lemon Balm – Joy and positive energy.

Add the base oil – 10x the total quantity of the other oils

Olive oil – Love and harmony.

Add a few:

Black peppercorns – Protection and cleansing of negative energy.

If possible, leave the oil in some sunlight for 20 minutes and ask the sun to charge it with fire energy for warmth, vitality and growth.

You can also leave it outside for the night to charge under the full moonlight. Call on the moon to enhance every aspect of the ingredients.

GOLDEN DRAGON SUCCESS & ABUNDANCE OIL.

Moon Phase: Full or waxing moon.

For financial abundance and work/venture success.

This oil can be adapted for other types of abundance and success. Just add an extra oil that corresponds with your needs.

Ingredients: Essential Oils – equal amounts of each:

Basil – Abundance and wealth.
Bay – Success and quick action.
Dragon Blood – Amplification and energy boost.
Lemon – Positivity and vitality.
Add the base oil – 10x the total quantity of the other oils.
Olive oil – Love and harmony.

Be mindful when making the oil that your abundance and gain does not harm anyone and will only be used to create a happy home and further enhance your resolve to bring a more enlightened world.

Add an image of the golden dragon of prosperity to your bottled oil. A charm tied around the neck of the bottle works well or it can be stuck to the top of the lid.

When you use the energy channelling exercise, envisage this beautiful shining dragon and she may just step in to help you.

If possible, leave the oil in some sunlight for 20 minutes and ask the sun to charge it with fire energy for positive action and thought.

You can also leave it outside for the night to charge under the full moonlight. Call in the moon to charge your oil and activate fully the intent of your ingredients.

DRAGON ROSE OIL.

For Love, Passion and Creativity.

Moon Phase: Full or waxing moon.

Use with a splash of water in an oil burner or diffuser whenever you need to create an environment for heightened sexual energy, increased fertility or during a love spell. The powerful vitality of the oils will also enhance any creativity and bring inspiration to artistic projects or kundalini yoga and meditations.

Dragons love creativity and vitality and will support your need for this powerful aspect of yourself. Sexual energy is the fundamental energy of life. It is a divine energy and the life force of every creature in every dimension. It fuels us in our need to survive, to create, to love and be loved.

Ingredients: Essential oils – equal amounts of each:

Rose – Love and creativity.
Ylang Ylang – Passion & aphrodisiac.
Dragon Blood – Amplification and energy boost.

Add the base oil – 10x the total quantity of the other oils.
Olive oil – Love and balance.

If possible, leave the oil in some sunlight for 20 minutes and ask the sun to charge it with fire energy for passion and creativity.

You can also leave it outside for the night to charge under the full moonlight.

Call in the moon to charge your oil and activate fully the powerful love intent of your ingredients.

A Blessing
for
Your Journey

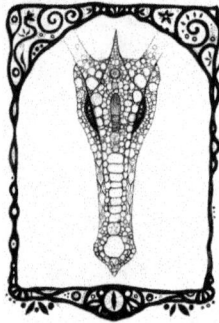

May your journey with Hearth Dragons be blessed with success, joy, opportunity, companionship and, above all, the hope of nurturing our New Earth.

www.ingramcontent.com/pod-product-compliance
Lightning Source LLC
Chambersburg PA
CBHW072012090426
42740CB00011B/2169